T0049222

Dictionary
of Fine
Distinctions

Dictionary *of* Fine Distinctions

Nuances, Niceties, and Subtle Shades of Meaning

An Assorted Synonymy & Encyclopedia

of Commonly Confused Objects, Ideas & Words,

Distinguished with the Aid of Illustrations

Eli Burnstein

ILLUSTRATED BY LIANA FINCK

UNION
SQUARE
& CO.

NEW YORK

Introduction, Foreword, *or* Preface

Which is it?

Everywhere we look, we're confronted by sneaky differences. That couch you're sitting on, is it more of a sofa? That cappuccino in your cup, how is it different from a flat white?

And it's not just the physical world, either. Do moral dilemmas differ from ethical ones? If we make an assumption, do we presume it as well? What about strategy and tactics? Proverbs and adages? Which of these terms is more accurate—or should we say, more *precise*?

With *Dictionary of Fine Distinctions*, we put life under the microscope, teasing irony apart from sarcasm, driving a wedge between gullies and ravines, exposing goblins, ogres, and trolls to the harsh sunlight of analysis. The result? Crisp, sparkling clarity.

Each entry offers a sort of mental taste test—a Pepsi Challenge, even— serving up two or more commonly confused phenomena and a brief description of what makes them different.

Thank God, there are also illustrations.

And not just any illustrations. Simple yet thoughtful, carefully wrought yet rippling with charm, they're the handiwork of the one and only Liana Finck, whose nervy lines have helped me to crystallize ideas in ways that words never could.

Of course, I should immediately clear my throat and say: Reality is messy. So while I have tried to single out differences as surgically as possible, regional variations in usage and the ever-shifting nature of language (not to mention my own fallibility) mean that I won't hit the bull's-eye for everyone at all times. Plus, some things are just fuzzy.

A final, dewy-eyed note: As you flip through the book, my hope is that you'll walk away not just with a clearer grasp of a hundred or so fine distinctions, but with a deeper appreciation for the inexhaustible subtlety of life—for the infinite and infinitesimal nuances that turn up everywhere we look. Louis MacNiece put it well, writing that

> *World is crazier and more of it than we think,*
> *Incorrigibly plural. I peel and portion*
> *A tangerine and spit the pips and feel*
> *The drunkenness of things being various.*

Eli Burnstein

P.S. Prefaces deal with incidental topics like the book's origin, scope, and limits, while introductions tend to kick off the subject matter proper and at greater length and generally feel more essential to the work.

Page numbers are a good giveaway: Standing outside the main text, prefaces usually feature lowercase Roman numerals (i, ii, iii) while introductions inaugurate the Arabic ones (1, 2, 3) that continue for the remainder of the book.

As you can tell, this is a preface.

Forewords, finally, are easier to spot, as they've been written by someone else—usually a well-known personage whose name is advertised on the cover to lend the book credibility. The most auxiliary of all, forewords come before prefaces, which, in turn, come before introductions.

Please don't hold the lack of a foreword against me.

Happy hairsplitting.

Emoji *vs.* Emoticon

EMOJI

Emojis are graphics.

;P

EMOTICON

Emoticons use type.

ADVANCED DISTINCTION

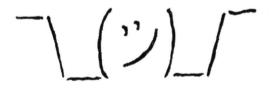

KAOMOJI

An upright and more elaborate style of
emoticon originating in Japan.

Symphony *vs.* Concerto

SYMPHONY

In a symphony, the whole orchestra
plays more or less together.

CONCERTO

In a concerto, a soloist plays somewhat apart from, and in dialogue with, the broader orchestra.

That's why it's often called a piano concerto or a violin concerto: The star instrument is explicitly called out.

Deep Web *vs.* Dark Web

DEEP WEB

The deep web refers to web pages that don't show up in search results but which may be viewed if you're logged in to the website in question.

DARK WEB

The dark web refers to websites accessible only through special anonymizing software and consisting largely of illegal activity.

The Fine Print

Deep web examples include email inboxes, personal banking account pages, company intranets, and the contents of academic and scientific databases.

Dark web examples include drug, weapons, data, and sex trafficking platforms; child pornography sites; and whistleblowing, activism, and communications tools for dissidents in countries where free speech is restricted.

It is estimated that the "surface web" makes up about 4 percent of the total content on the internet, while 90 percent is the deep web and 6 percent the dark web, though estimates vary.

Great Britain *vs.* United Kingdom

GREAT BRITAIN

Great Britain is a geographical term referring to a single island or landmass.

UNITED KINGDOM

The United Kingdom is a political term referring to the country made up of England, Scotland, and Wales (which together make up Great Britain), together with Northern Ireland.

Envy *vs.* Jealousy

Envy is when you want something that someone else has.

Jealousy is when you *don't* want others to have something—or someone—that you do.

I envy Mark's physique.

We were just hanging out. Stop being so jealous!

To Have and Have Not

Envy is an unhappy longing for the possessions or qualities of others, while jealousy is an excessive guarding of the attentions one currently enjoys—whether love, sex, or friendship—typified by an undue suspicion of others and possessiveness over the person or people granting those attentions. Even God, who wants all the worship to himself, gets jealous:

You shall not bow down to them or serve them, for I the Lord . . . am a jealous God.

—Exodus 20:5

USAGE NOTE

Despite the protestations of some, jealous can also be used to mean envious (*You're going to France? Jealous.*) and has a centuries-old record of doing so. This makes sense when you consider that the two terms' opposing positions—one of wanting but not having, the other of having but risking losing to another—are often slippery and interchangeable.

Bay *vs.* Gulf *vs.* Cove

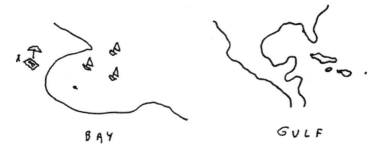

Bays are recessed bodies of water.

Gulfs are very large bays.

A small bay, usually with a narrow entrance and sheltered by steep cliff walls.

Latte *vs.* Flat White *vs.* Cappuccino *vs.* Cortado

LATTE

FLAT WHITE

All four espresso drinks contain steamed milk, but in different amounts: Lattes are the largest and milkiest, while cortados are the smallest and strongest.

Where things get complicated is with the middle two. Cappuccinos might be slightly bigger than flat whites or vice versa—or, gallingly, one might contain a single rather than double shot of espresso—but plenty of coffee shops make them the exact same way.

The one difference worth noting, however, has to do with foam: Baristas tend to stretch the milk in flat whites only around 20 to 30 percent, while for cappuccinos they may go as high as 40 or even 50 percent. The result? Cappuccinos are often fluffier in texture, which means that where cup size and espresso volume remain constant, they taste stronger too.

Stretch?

Stretching is barista slang for aerating the milk, which is when you raise the steam wand to the surface of the milk to gently whisk in a little air. The difference, then, is that with a cappuccino, you *might* stretch the milk a few seconds longer, resulting in a fluffier liquid that, by virtue of its increased volume, doesn't cut the espresso as much.

CAPPUCCINO

CORTADO

That, at least, is the quasi-difference when both drinks are made with microfoam: the flat, white, silky-looking froth that comes standard on all flat whites (hence the name) and on 99 percent of cappuccinos found in most trendy coffee shops today. But if you're bucking the microfoam trend, there's always the dry foam cappuccino of old, which is produced by bringing the spout a touch higher (and holding it there for longer) to introduce air more vigorously into the milk, resulting in those large-bubbled billows we all remember from the '90s. Bone-dry cappuccinos, a rare extreme, are all foam and no milk: a pillow on a black pond. Note, however, that these misshapen crowns are for cappuccinos only: The "dry foam flat white" is an impossible object.

Surface Foam *vs.* Textured Milk

But there's one more piece to the puzzle: blending. Contrary to those diagrams of espresso drinks you sometimes see—where foam, milk, and espresso are laid out in distinct strips—a good flat white or latter-day cappuccino actually mixes all three together. That's because, once your expert barista aerates the milk, they will subsequently plunge the wand farther down

---

into the pitcher to create a whirlpool, effectively blending the foam they just made with the steaming milk below. The result? A thick, velvety, textured milk from top to bottom, which is then poured over the espresso.

Almost immediately, however, the textured milk will begin to separate, forming a head of surface foam that also gets progressively drier. And because there's often more air in a cappuccino to begin with (see above), over time you'll see it form a larger head (~1 cm) than that of a flat white (~5 mm). So while those diagrams of layered liquids unfairly write textured milk out of the story, they at least show you what you'd get if you left your drink untouched for way too long.

Assume *vs.* Presume

ASSUME

To assume is to suppose without proof.

I assumed you knew where you were going!

PRESUME

To presume is to do so with confidence or authority.

Your daughter, I presume?

The Fine Print

Assume and presume both mean to suppose, believe, or take for granted that something is true despite a lack of hard proof. Yet presuming is more confident because it suggests that there's at least *some* good evidence for the thing believed: *When the boat washed up empty, he was presumed dead*. Assuming, by contrast, is based on weaker grounds for belief, or none at all, and thus lacks the swagger of presumption: *You assume incorrectly—I'm Belgian*.

Accuracy *vs.* Precision

ACCURACY

Accuracy refers to how close you are to the correct answer.

PRECISION

Precision refers to how closely or finely you're measuring.

EXAMPLE

A jar has 76 jelly beans in it. David guesses there are 125. Lucy guesses there are between 50 and 100. David is precise but not accurate; Lucy is accurate but not precise.

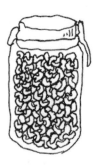

Technically Speaking

In the sciences, these terms have more technical—but ultimately similar—meanings to their everyday counterparts: Accuracy refers to how close your readings are to an object's true value, while precision refers to how close your readings are to one another, i.e., how *consistent* they are.

The distinction is useful in diagnosing different kinds of error: Accurate but imprecise readings suggest your tools are too coarse—you need a yardstick that can measure in eighth inches rather than quarter inches—while precise but inaccurate readings may mean your tools are poorly calibrated—your yardstick isn't quite a yard, and it's introducing systemic bias into your results.

TARGET PRACTICE

- Precise but inaccurate archers are off the mark but consistently so: A slight tweak in their angle and they'll be pros.
- Imprecise but accurate archers are on the mark but only roughly so: With practice and focus, they'll start hitting the bull's-eye dead-on.
- Archers who are both imprecise and inaccurate are bad at archery.

Ethics *vs.* Morality

ETHICS

MORALITY

Ethics refers to intelligible principles of right and wrong.

Code of ethics
Workplace ethics

Morality refers to right and wrong as *a felt sense*.

Moral compass
Moral fiber

One is rational, explicit, and defined by one's social or professional community; the other is emotional, deep-seated, and dictated by one's conscience or god.

That's why an immoral act sounds graver than an unethical one: One may get you fired, but the other could land you in hell.

The Fine Print

With characteristic sass, usage master H. W. Fowler notes that "The two words, once fully synonymous, & existing together only because English scholars knew both Greek & Latin [ethics being Greek in origin, morality Latin], have so far divided functions that neither is superfluous . . . *ethics* is the science of morals, & *morals* are the practice of ethics."*

While Fowler is here alluding to ethics as a branch of philosophy, the conceptual flavor of the word can be heard in its everyday sense as well: Whether theorized by Aristotle or spelled out in a code of conduct, ethics is morality, as it were, with glasses on.

---

* H. W. Fowler, *A Dictionary of Modern English Usage*, 1st ed. (Oxford, UK: Clarendon Press, 1926), 152.

Tights *vs.* Leggings *vs.* Pantyhose *vs.* Stockings

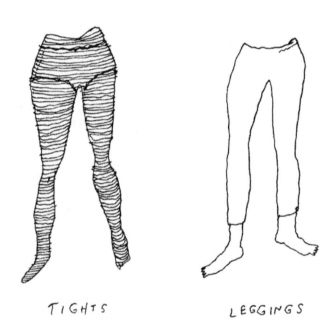

TIGHTS

LEGGINGS

Tights cover the feet. Leggings, as their name suggests, don't. Tights are also an undergarment and so tend to be thinner and somewhat sheer, whereas leggings can be thicker and worn as pants all on their own.

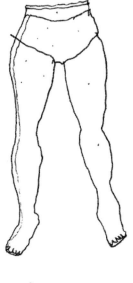

PANTYHOSE

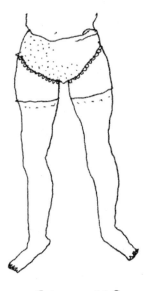

STOCKINGS

Pantyhose are an extra-sheer form of tights, often with more opaque fabric covering the upper or "panty" portion of the panty/hose combination that their name suggests.

Less common today, stockings are detached undergarments that stop around the thigh. Sort of like the ones hanging over the fireplace at Christmas.

First Cousin *vs.* Once Removed

First cousins have the same grandparents. Second cousins have the same great-grandparents. In general, degree of cousinhood is determined by distance to a common ancestor.

Once removed means you're a generation apart. Twice removed means you're two generations apart. In general, degree of removal is determined by the generational difference between the two cousins themselves.

In short, when you hear "third cousin," you're about to meet someone you're barely related to, but when you hear "thrice removed," you're about to meet someone astoundingly old.

MNEMONIC 1: HORIZONTALITY

Cousinhood is horizontal. Removalhood is vertical. If you don't hear the word "removed," you're in the same generation.

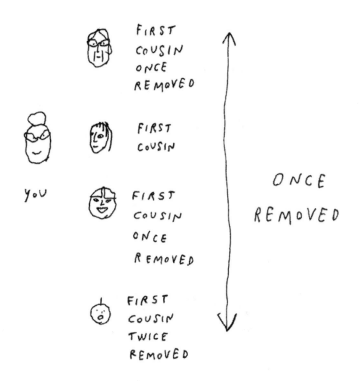

FIRST COUSIN ONCE REMOVED

FIRST COUSIN

YOU

FIRST COUSIN ONCE REMOVED

ONCE REMOVED

FIRST COUSIN TWICE REMOVED

MNEMONIC 2: THE G RULE

To establish degree of cousinhood, simply count the number of g's before finding a shared ancestor: Same grandparents? First cousins. Same great-grandparents? Second cousins. And so on . . . And if you're of different generations, simply pick the smaller number of g's between you: If my grandparents are your great-grandparents, we're first cousins—and because of the single generational difference between us, we're also once removed.

Shame *vs.* Guilt

SHAME

You feel shame for not being good enough.

GUILT

You feel guilt for not doing the right thing.

Who You Are *vs.* What You Do

Shame is the feeling that your innate qualities don't live up to the standards of beauty, intelligence, character, etc., as defined by your peers or society.

Guilt, by contrast, is the feeling that the actions or thoughts over which you have control transgress standards of right and wrong as dictated by the law, your parents, your conscience, or your god.

One is about who you are and are not, the other about what you do or don't do: I feel ashamed of my puny muscles—and guilty for not going to the gym.

Autocrat *vs.* Despot *vs.* Tyrant *vs.* Dictator

Autocrats rule with absolute power. Despots rule with absolute power cruelly and oppressively. Tyrants rule with absolute power cruelly, oppressively, and illegitimately (usurper). Dictators rule with absolute power cruelly, oppressively, and under a newly established regime.

The Fine Print

- An autocrat rules with absolute power by legitimate means, often within a long-standing or established political system such as a monarchy. Of the four terms, autocrat carries the least negative connotation, though it's still widely considered undesirable.
  ARCHETYPE: Czar Nicholas II of Russia

- A despot rules with absolute power by legitimate means, but oppressively so, and often within a long-standing political order where the domination of the ruler and the unfreedom of its people is the norm. Carrying a regrettable hint of orientalism, the term has historically been used by Western nations in reference to leaders of countries elsewhere—a counterpoint, as it were, to the freedom of one's own state.
  ARCHETYPE: Pharaoh Ramesses II of Ancient Egypt

- Unlike the first two rulers, whose sovereignty is sanctioned by law or custom, tyrants are illegitimate usurpers, seizing the reins by nefarious means. And while despots may hold entire peoples under their thumb as a matter of course, tyrants add an extra measure of frenzied, paranoia-fueled cruelty toward perceived rivals and political threats.
  ARCHETYPE: Macbeth, King of Scotland

  O nation miserable,
  With an untitled tyrant bloody-sceptered,
  When shalt thou see thy wholesome days again . . . ?

  —*Macbeth*, act 4, scene 3

- A dictator, finally, rules with self-legitimizing power within a recently established (rather than long-standing) political order, which is why a dictator is typically not a monarch (tyrants aren't so picky). Here, too, cruelty and oppression are the norm, drawing on ideology, propaganda, and militarization to convert its people from the old way of doing things to the wholly new regime. **ARCHETYPE: Adolf Hitler, Führer of Nazi Germany**

ORIGINAL MEANINGS

In the Roman Republic, the term *dictator* referred to an individual temporarily granted extraordinary powers in a state of emergency—but when Julius Caesar was pronounced *dictator perpetuo*, the original meaning of the term was perverted, prefiguring the doublespeak of modern dictatorships (e.g., "president for life").

Tyrant, meanwhile, originally referred to usurpers but not necessarily bad ones—maybe they deposed a despot.

Typeface *vs.* Font

Helvetica

Arial

Courier

Garamond

Comic Sans

Helvetica Light

Helvetica Regular

Helvetica Italic

Helvetica Bold

Helvetica Bold Italic

Helvetica, Arial, and Courier are typefaces.

Helvetica Light, Arial Italics, and Courier Bold are fonts.

One refers to a typographical design system, the other to one of its many weights (light to **heavy**) or styles (roman, **boldface**, *italic*, condensed, etc.). A typeface is a family; a font is one of its members.

USAGE NOTE

Outside the world of typography, the use of font to mean typeface is so common that the error, if it can even be called one, is likely here to stay. Given that font is easier to say, that might not be such a bad thing.

You are currently reading the Regular font of the Brandon Grotesque typeface. The main text above is Meno Display Regular.

Snitch *vs.* Rat

SNITCH

A snitch informs on others (tattletale).

RAT

A rat sells out their own (traitor).

When Randy Wagstaff tells the assistant principal who sprayed graffiti at school, he's a snitch. When Cypher betrays captain Morpheus to Agent Smith, he's a rat.

A Tale of Two Rats

Note that the term rat may refer to an actual traitor *or* to an undercover agent who, though never really part of the group to begin with, nevertheless embeds with them and eventually breaks their trust. The former we may call true rats (Cypher, Judas), the latter false rats or moles (Donnie Brasco, Billy Costigan).

MORE SNITCHES
- Randall Weems
- Reginald "Bubbles" Cousins

MORE TRUE RATS
- Pussy Bonpensiero
- Fredo Corleone

MORE FALSE RATS (MOLES)
- Colin Sullivan
- Mr. Orange

Epigram *vs.* Aphorism *vs.* Maxim *vs.* Adage *vs.* Proverb

EPIGRAM

Epigrams are witty.

"One should always play fairly . . . when one has the winning cards."

—Mrs. Cheveley, in Oscar Wilde's *An Ideal Husband*

APHORISM

Aphorisms are philosophical.

"Even the bravest of us rarely has the courage for what he really knows."

—Friedrich Nietzsche, *Twilight of the Idols*

MAXIM

Maxims are rules of conduct.

"Know thyself."

—Inscribed in the Temple of Apollo at Delphi

ADAGE

Adages are old and well-known.

"The best defense is a good offense."

PROVERB

Proverbs are folk/traditional.

"A bird in the hand is worth two in the bush."

—English Proverb

The first two tend to be attributable to an individual writer, the latter three less so, but really, these categories are defined so loosely, and their potential for overlap is so great, that your best bet is just to try to say something clever and let others decide.

Adages of Old

Incidentally, given that all adages are old, or at least are supposed to be, the phrase *old adage* is considered by many usage experts to be redundant. Yet it's a pairing that goes back centuries, proving that our love of emphasis (or the charm of alliteration) makes bad logicians of us all.

> *"I might repeat to myself, slowly and soothingly,*
> *a list of quotations beautiful from minds profound;*
> *if I can remember any of the damn things."*

—Dorothy Parker (epigram)

Natural Numbers *vs.* Integers *vs.* Rational Numbers *vs.* Real Numbers

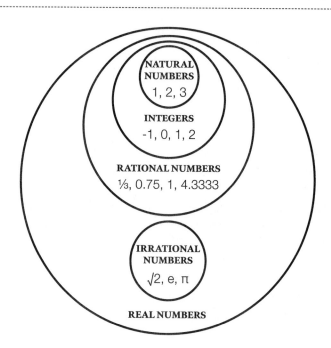

1, 2, 3, and so on are natural numbers. Add negatives and you've got integers. Add fractions or their expression as decimal numbers and you've got rational numbers. Finally, add non-terminating, non-repeating decimal numbers like π (3.14159 . . .) and √2 (1.24348 . . .), otherwise known as irrational numbers, and you've got the set of all real numbers.

Zero Debate

Natural numbers are sometimes referred to as "counting numbers," which is nice and intuitive (1 cow, 2 cows). Annoyingly, however, some number systems include 0 among the set of natural numbers, which kind of messes up the whole counting thing. (Can you count no cows? Not really.) Yet other systems fare no better, for by relegating 0 to a slightly broader set called whole numbers, they make the whole thing needlessly complicated. This insoluble dilemma is, I'm sure, a source of endless frustration to the mathematics community.

Also: Rational numbers are so called because they're made up of *ratios* of two integers, aka fractions. Irrational numbers, by contrast, cannot be reduced to such ratios—they are incommensurable. Hence the never-ending randomness.

ADVANCED DISTINCTION

Imaginary Numbers

Beyond the universe of real numbers lies an exotic category of hypothetical oddities called imaginary numbers ($\sqrt{-1}$, shortened to i), which, together with real numbers, form an extended set known as complex numbers.

Squash *vs.* Racquetball

SQUASH

In squash, you hit a firm ball with a narrow racket.

RACQUETBALL

In racquetball, you hit a bouncy ball with a fat racket.

If you remember one of them, make it squash: It's much more popular.

Cube Sports

Both sports are played in an enclosed, four-walled space by either two players or four. In racquetball, though, the racket's a bit shorter and wider, the ball's a bit bigger and bouncier, and the court's a bit longer and higher.

There are a handful of other differences, too, including how you serve (volley vs. bounce serve), how scoring works (per rally vs. per served rally), and, most importantly, what counts as out of bounds: In squash, the ball can't hit the ceiling, upper walls, or a strip of metal at the bottom called the "tin." In racquetball, it's comparatively open season.

Between the ball, racket, and playable surface area, racquetball is arguably a bit easier to pick up, though squash is far more popular.

Oh, and there's a third sport called racketball (note the spelling) that in its rules, equipment, and dimensions falls somewhere between the other two. To confuse matters even more, it was recently renamed "squash 57."

FRASIER: Bulldog, have you met my brother Niles? Niles, this is Bulldog Briscoe.

NILES: Oh, oh, oh. Just the man I want to talk to. As a sports expert I'm sure you can tell me why none of the local media carry the Ivy League squash standings.

BULLDOG: [*laughing*] Whoa! Another one just like you.

—*Frasier*, season 2, episode 13

Flail *vs.* Mace *vs.* Morning Star

FLAIL

Flails have a chain.

MACE

Maces don't.

MORNING STAR

Morning stars are spiked maces. Oof.

Putting It Bluntly

Despite the image of flails we get from the movies—as short-handled, long-chained, and with a ball for its business end—most were in fact long-handled, short-chained (or hinged), and struck their unhappy victims with a cylindrical bar of wood. This makes sense when you consider that the flail was originally a two-handed agricultural tool used for beating wheat berries and other edible grains out of their stalks and husks, an activity otherwise known as threshing.

AGRICULTURAL FLAIL

The business end of a farming flail is called a swipple.

MNEMONIC

Flails flail.

Kitsch *vs.* Camp

Kitsch is tacky art and design.

Camp is over-the-top film, TV, and performance.

Kitschy lamp.

Campy horror film.

Kitsch may be used pejoratively or as a term of ironic appreciation. Camp is a term of appreciation through and through.

The Fine Print

Both styles deviate from traditional notions of good taste, but in different ways.

Kitsch refers to art and design that's considered garish, cutesy, cheap, nostalgic, or sentimental. Though largely a term of abuse, kitsch may be applied to such artworks when enjoyed (or even produced) ironically. Your grandmother's piglet figurines are classic kitsch, but so are your beloved tiki mugs.

Camp, by contrast, is never pejorative, but refers to such garishness only when made or enjoyed knowingly. The term is especially used in reference to screen and stage performances marked by unrestrained theatricality and playful extravagance. *The Rocky Horror Picture Show* is iconic camp, as are episodes of 1960s *Batman* and, unintentionally, *The Room*. The camp aesthetic grew out of gay culture and, though indulged far and wide, remains closely associated with it.

KITSCH

- Garden gnomes
- Lava lamps
- Tiki bars
- Framed photographs of white-walled homes in Santorini
- Anything at a souvenir shop
- Big Mouth Billy Bass (talking fish)
- Muzak

CAMP

- Lady Gaga
- *Army of Darkness*
- KISS
- *Pink Flamingos*
- B-movies
- *Batman* (1966)
- *The Addams Family*
- *Hairspray* (1988 and 2007)
- *Jesus Christ Superstar*

"Kitsch is the epitome of all that is spurious in the life of our times."
—Clement Greenberg, "Avant-Garde and Kitsch," 1939

"The whole point of Camp is to dethrone the serious."
—Susan Sontag, "Notes on Camp," 1964

Amp *vs.* Volt *vs.* Watt

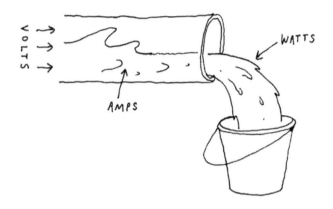

Amps tell you the amount of electricity.
Volts tell you the pressure of electricity.
Watts tell you the output of electricity.

The Fine Print

Electricity is like water flowing through a tap: The amps indicate how much electrical current is actually flowing through the wires in a given period of time, while the volts indicate the pressure at which that current is being pushed. Wattage, finally, measures the amount of power actually generated and is simply the product of the first two terms.

Amps x Volts = Watts

In short, when you hear amps, think current, when you hear volts, think pressure, and when you hear watts, think utility bill.

Cardinal Number *vs.* Ordinal Number

1, 2, 3

CARDINAL NUMBER

Cardinal numbers
are for counting.

Three sheets.

1st, 2nd, 3rd

ORDINAL NUMBER

Ordinal numbers
are for ordering.

Third inning.

Sorbet *vs.* Sherbet

SORBET

Sorbet is nondairy.

SHERBET

Sherbet may add
up to 2% milkfat.

The Fine Print

Sherbet, unlike sorbet, may also add egg or gelatin, and in general tends to be smoother and creamier than sorbet due to its higher fat content. Sherbets are almost always served as desserts, whereas sorbet is served either as a dessert or as a palate cleanser between courses. Sherbert, with an additional *r*, is a variant spelling (and pronunciation) considered by many to be incorrect, though its use has been attested as early as 1675.

Convince *vs.* Persuade

CONVINCE

You convince someone to believe something.

Zoe convinced Michael
of the existence of God.

PERSUADE

You persuade someone to *do* something.

Then she persuaded him
to go to church.

A Dying Distinction

Strictly speaking, the distinction is a grammatical one, the principle being that *convince* should pair with *of* plus a noun, while *persuade* should pair with *to* plus a verb. But the outcome of such verbal associations is that convince tends to refer to matters of thought (*convince me of the need*), persuade to matters of action (*persuade me to vote*).

You may wish to observe this rule to keep your writing nice and crisp, but these days the distinction is so subdued, and the two words' interchangeability so accepted, that they may be treated as more or less equivalent.

Catapult *vs.* Trebuchet

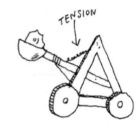

TENSION

CATAPULT

Catapults hurl objects through a sudden release of tension.

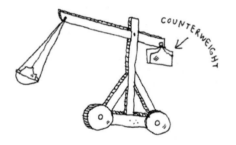

COUNTERWEIGHT

TREBUCHET

Trebuchets hurl objects through counterweights and a sling.

Trebuchets are better.

The Fine Print

Okay so technically they're all catapults, and the one on the left is properly called an onager. But no one knows the word onager, and generally when people think of catapults they think of the one on top at left (despite the trebuchet's superiority in both payload weight and distance).

I fear the revenge of the nerds, so I should also note that onagers eventually swapped out their bucket for a sling (similar to that of the trebuchet), giving it further range. Despite how they're usually depicted, onagers also tended not to have wheels but were rooted firmly in place because of their powerful recoil.

Finally, though our onager features a spring to illustrate that its source of power lies in tension, that tension is actually created from a stretch of twisted ropes hugging the base of the projectile arm: The lower the projectile arm is cranked, the stronger the tension in those ropes gets. More technically still, this kind of twisting force isn't called tension but torsion.

There are other types of catapults too, like ballistae (giant crossbows) and mangonels (trebuchets that use people pulling ropes instead of a counterweight), all of them more or less obsolete.

Goblin *vs.* Ogre *vs.* Troll

GOBLIN

Goblins are small
and devilish.

OGRE

Ogres are big
and brutish.

TROLL

Trolls are weird and reclusive—
the wildest of the bunch.

Beast Mode

Goblins are funny-looking little sprites that often hang around people's homes, playing tricks that range from charmingly impish to outright demonic. (Hobgoblin, a variant, suggests a being on the friendlier end of that spectrum.) Related creatures include the German kobold and the Korean dokkaebi.

Ogres are big-boned and mean as hell. Known to be good eaters, some of them will feast on humans for dinner, especially babies. Ogres share a mythological lineage with giants. Hence the eating humans thing.

Trolls, finally, can be found in far-off caves or hills, away from human civilization. Trolls come from Norse mythology and Scandinavian folklore, and, over the centuries, have been described in so many ways that it's hard to keep track: large, small, dangerous, dumb, old, magical, prophetic, shape-shifting, kidnapping, turning to stone in the sun, and living under and/or controlling bridges.

Variations aside, the troll's signature difference from the others seems to be a sort of shaggy remoteness from human civilization: They're said to be encountered only deep in nature.

Also, none of them are necessarily green.

Porch *vs.* Deck *vs.* Veranda *vs.* Pati

P O R C H

Porches are covered shelters projecting
from a building's front or back entrance.

D E C K

Decks are like porches, only larger, uncovered, and
always made of wood. They tend to sit at the back.

VERANDA

Verandas are porches that run along the length of a building or wrap around it and which are marked by recurring pillars.

PATIO

Patios, finally, are paved open patches that adjoin buildings at ground level—in other words, lower than the other three.

Club Soda *vs.* Sparkling Water *vs.* Seltzer

CLUB SODA

SPARKLING WATER

SELTZER

Club soda is water that's been artificially carbonated and to which mineral salts have been added for flavor.

Sparkling water, or more specifically sparkling *mineral* water, is what club soda is trying to imitate: naturally effervescent and minerally balanced water that wells up ready to drink right out of the spring—think Perrier or San Pellegrino—though here, too, some processing is involved.

Seltzer, finally, refers to water that's been artificially carbonated but which has no mineral salts added, leaving it less savory and more acidic than its club soda counterpart. The simple makeup of seltzer—water plus carbon dioxide—makes it a good neutral backdrop for flavored fizzies like LaCroix.

More Terms

Sparkling water and soda water are umbrella terms for carbonated water, yet there's a distinction here, too: Sparkling water suggests a drink to be enjoyed on its own (as in the phrase "still or sparkling?"), whereas soda water suggests a mixer to be added to drinks (as in the drink scotch and soda).

Tonic water, finally, is a sugary soft drink containing quinine and best paired with gin. It's something else entirely.

The Takeaway

If you're going to drink it on its own, shell out for the mineral stuff or satisfy yourself with club; unless it's flavored or you plan to flavor it yourself, seltzers won't have as much going on.

As for drinks simply labeled "sparkling water" or "soda water," check the label to see if they're a plain and humble seltzer or salty, mid-range club. Unless they say otherwise, you can safely rule out mineral—they'd be sure to brag about that.

ADVANCED DISTINCTION

Mineral vs. Spring

Among the higher-end waters—carbonated or otherwise—there's a slight difference between those that say "mineral" and those labeled "spring." To claim the lofty term mineral in the US, the water needs to have at least 250 parts per million of naturally occurring protected underground minerals dissolved in the water, with none added after the fact—otherwise, it doesn't make the cut.

Hermit *vs.* Anchorite

HERMIT

A hermit retires from society to live alone in the wilderness.

ANCHORITE

An anchorite retires from society to live in an enclosed cell attached to a church.

One lives apart. The other, within.

Eclectic Ascetics

Hermit dwellings, or hermitages, can be as simple and remote as a cave in the desert, or as developed and nearby as a detached building on monastery property.

Historically, anchorages (or anchor-holds) were attached to churches in the center of town, the individuals dwelling within them serving as spiritual guides for the community. In the late Middle Ages, female anchorites (or anchoresses) far outnumbered male ones.

It's worth noting that during an anchorite's walling-in ceremony, a bishop or local priest would read them their funeral rites: They were to be considered "dead to the world."

Stylites, finally, were an early and extreme type of ascetic who would live at the top of a column or pillar for years or even decades—most of the time standing.

Maze *vs.* Labyrinth

MAZE

LABYRINTH

A maze has many paths and challenges you to find the exit.

A labyrinth has one path and draws you toward its center.

One is a puzzle designed to challenge and amuse.
The other is an exercise designed to calm down the mind.

Walking in Circles

Labyrinths have served a variety of ritual and religious purposes over the millennia, from traps for evil spirits, to burial grounds, to crucibles of personal transformation and symbols of the path to salvation. Wherever they pop up, the idea, in part, seems to be that the repetitive and uncomplicated motion of walking in spiral-like formations can bring on a relaxed, even contemplative frame of mind. Hence the labyrinth's modern therapeutic appeal.

EXCEPTION

The eponymous labyrinth of ancient Greek mythology—the one with the ferocious Minotaur in its depths—is, in descriptions by classical authors, pretty obviously a maze. Otherwise, why would Theseus need to retrace his steps with a length of thread after slaying the monster? Shouldn't it be easy (albeit tedious) to get out?

Verdict

Greek namesakes notwithstanding, there remains a meaningful difference between a forking navigational game that's riddled with dead ends and a winding hypnotic track that isn't. Mazes refer to the first kind of object; labyrinths, alas, are a bit either/or.

SARAH: You're a worm aren't you?
WORM: Yeah, s'right.
SARAH: You don't by any chance know the way through this labyrinth do you?
WORM: Who me? Naaah, I'm just a worm.

—From *Labyrinth* (1986)

All-Wheel Drive (AWD) *vs.* Four-Wheel Drive (4WD)

ALL-WHEEL DRIVE (AWD)

AWD is for on-roading in slippery conditions.

FOUR-WHEEL DRIVE (4WD)

4WD is for off-roading in extreme terrain.

One is safe and sophisticated. The other, rugged and badass.

Each *vs.* Every

AWD is an automatic, always-on system that intelligently distributes power to front and rear wheels as needed, making it great for wet roads and light off-roading, but also hard turns, precision steering, and performance driving more generally.

4WD, by contrast, is a manual, on/off system that (when on) rigidly equalizes power distribution to all four wheels, delivering the hard-core traction needed to traverse mud, sand, rivers, boulders—you name it.

Robbery *vs.* Burglary

ROBBERY

Robbery is theft from a person by force or threat.

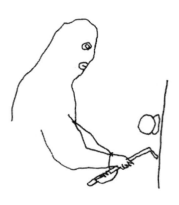

BURGLARY

Burglary is theft from a building by illegal entry.

Department of Corrections

As it happens, you don't actually need to commit theft for your actions to qualify as burglary. Any felony, even any *intention* of a felony—arson, murder, etc.—will do, so long as you unlawfully enter a building to do so.

ADVANCED DISTINCTION

Larceny

Larceny is an umbrella term referring to all manner of personal property theft—including robbery and burglaries involving theft (see above), but also pickpocketing, purse-snatching, and shoplifting. Though conceptually similar to theft, larceny tends to be a bit narrower in scope, referring to tangible possessions and not, say, identity theft.

Spear *vs.* Javelin *vs.* Lance *vs.* Pike

SPEAR

Spears are thrust.

JAVELIN

Javelins are hurled.

LANCE

Lances are charged with on horseback.

PIKE

Pikes are held with two hands in line formation, often against lance-bearing cavalry. They're very long.

Putting It Sharply

Over the millennia, polearms have assumed a variety of forms, crisscrossing into a bit of a blur. The pilum, for instance, was a long and heavy javelin designed to pierce shields, while the dory was a line-formation spear tipped at both ends (subsequently lengthened to the more pikelike sarissa). Given the profusion of types, *spear* has come to be used as an umbrella term referring to the long-and-stabby category of polearms as a whole—as opposed to, say, long-and-slashy ones like the halberd.

Dinner *vs.* Supper

Dinner is the largest meal of the day.

DINNER

Supper is lighter evening fare eaten in rural areas where dinner is traditionally consumed at midday.

SUPPER

Urban	**Rural**
Breakfast	Breakfast
Lunch	Dinner
Dinner	Supper

Dinner Deferred

Before the industrial revolution, farmers would eat their largest meal late in the morning or early in the afternoon to keep themselves fueled for the demands of preindustrial farming. Then, in the evening, they would top themselves up with a lighter meal called supper, usually just some cold leftovers or something simmering on the stove from earlier in the day (*soup* and *supper* being related words).

Why did our biggest meal shift to later in the day? The short answer is urbanization, which over the course of the nineteenth century drew more and more workers away from their farms and into factories, offices, etc., making it harder to duck out and have a proper meal until later. A big midday meal also became unnecessary as industrialization made work progressively less toilsome and calorie-intensive. Still, that's a long time to wait between breakfast and dinner, so we invented something quick to tide us over in the meantime: lunch.

Farming-dominant regions in the American South and Midwest, meanwhile, followed a different evolution in their meal plans. Unlike their urban counterparts, farmers continued to work close to home and so could hold on to their midday dinners for longer. Yet at the same time, the onset of labor-saving machinery led many of these communities to shrink (rather than defer) those dinners, leading to a peculiar reversal in which dinner became smaller than supper, though many have stopped calling it dinner and conceded to the newfangled language of lunch.

Parable *vs.* Fable

PARABLE

A parable is a brief tale with a moral lesson.

FABLE

A fable is a brief tale with a moral lesson—plus animals.

Tales That Teach

Fables personify animals to illustrate a point about human folly, as for instance in the fable of the tortoise and the hare. Because of their dissociation from humans, fables tend to be lighter, more ironic fare.

Parables, by contrast, feature humans, and try to convey a deeper or more complex message about the human condition. In the case of Jesus's parable of the prodigal son, for instance, the message is that it is better to be forgiving than to be just, or that God loves sinners, or that . . . well, it's complex.

A person who writes fables is a fabulist.

Continental US *vs.* Contiguous US

CONTINENTAL US

CONTIGUOUS US

The Continental US includes all states on the North American continent. In other words, everything but Hawaii.

The Contiguous US includes all states that are contiguous, i.e., touching. In other words, everything but Hawaii and Alaska.

Altered States

The Contiguous US is officially known as the Conterminous US, but no one actually calls it that. It's also colloquially referred to as the Lower 48, which is a bit inaccurate given the southerly latitude of Hawaii.

Shotgun House *vs.* Railroad Apartment

A shotgun house* is a narrow, single-story home common in the American South, especially New Orleans.

A railroad apartment is a narrow unit design common among the old tenement buildings of NYC.

In both floor plans, one room leads directly to the next. Sort of like a shotgun barrel, or cars on a railway train.

The Fine Print

Without a hallway running parallel to connect each room, these straight-line layouts offer little to no privacy, especially—as with many tenements in the nineteenth and early twentieth centuries—when more than one family lived in a single unit.

* Also called a shotgun shack.

UI *vs.* UX

UI

UI refers to an application's surface aesthetic.

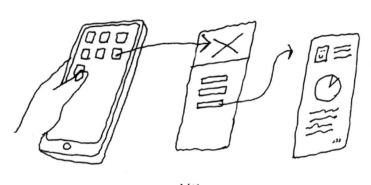

UX

UX refers to its deeper navigability.

The Fine Print

User interface (UI) designers combine shapes, colors, and fonts to create an enjoyable look and feel. User experience (UX) designers build customer journey maps to determine the various paths a user may take to get where they need to go.

Note that both designers are responsible for keeping things intuitive and clear, but in different ways: UI is about making sure users recognize buttons and other elements for what they are, that spacing and color contrasts aren't disorienting or harsh, and so on; UX, by contrast, is about determining the order, number, and interrelationship of pages such that the user remains oriented on their journey throughout the app.

Some writers argue that UI is a subtype of UX, and that UX refers to both. But that strikes me as needlessly complicated—in effect, bad UX.

Combination *vs.* Permutation

Ordering a burger, fries, and a soft drink is a combination: You're forming one of many possible groups.

COMBINATION

Asking for the fries to come before the burger is a permutation: You're ordering that group in one of many possible ways.

PERMUTATION

With combinations, order doesn't matter.
With permutations, it does.

A Dinner Party

Your guest list is a combination because it's a particular group of people. Your seating chart is a permutation because it's a particular arrangement of that group.

Balcony *vs.* Terrace

Balconies are projecting platforms.

BALCONY

Terraces are raised platforms.

TERRACE

Out *vs.* Up

Balconies jut out from buildings at upper-floor levels and are supported by brackets (as shown at left), pillars, suspended chains, or nothing (cantilevered).

Terraces, by contrast, are raised up from the ground—whether as high as the roof or as low as a few inches above the earth—and are supported by the building itself. They tend to be larger than balconies.

Speedometer *vs.* Odometer

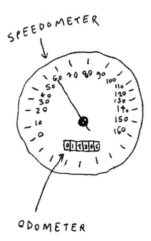

SPEEDOMETER

ODOMETER

Speedometers measure speed.

Odometers measure distance.

ADVANCED DISTINCTION

Tachometers measure the revolutions per minute (RPMs) of your car's engine, and in particular of the crankshaft turning the pistons inside it. That's why increasing your car's RPMs is called "revving the engine."

TACHOMETER

Blank Verse *vs.* Free Verse

Blank verse is poetry that doesn't rhyme.

Free verse is poetry that doesn't rhyme or have a regular rhythm.

Poetry Unbound

Blank verse is poetry that doesn't rhyme but which follows a regular meter, most commonly iambic pentameter. Used by Shakespeare, Milton, Wordsworth, and many other prominent English-speaking poets, blank verse is arguably the most common poetic form in the English language.

Thus Satan talking to his nearest mate
With head uplift above the wave, and eyes
That sparkling blazed; his other parts besides
Prone on the flood, extended long and large . . .

—John Milton, from *Paradise Lost*, book 1

Free verse, by contrast, isn't just unrhymed but unmetered, resulting in a looser, more natural poetic style than even blank verse had been able to achieve in relation to rhymed verse. Though it has antecedents stretching back to the Hebrew Psalms, free verse emerged as a distinct form in the late nineteenth century, and has been popular ever since.

Whirl up, sea—
whirl your pointed pines,
splash your great pines
on our rocks,
hurl your green over us,
cover us with your pools of fir.

—H.D., "Oread"

Crypt *vs.* Catacomb

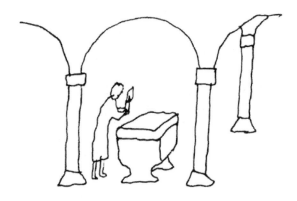

CRYPT

Crypts house the dead in vaulted chambers under churches.

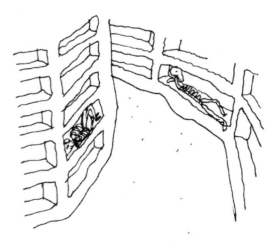

CATACOMB

Catacombs house the dead in
extensive networks under cities.

One is an underground tomb for the few,
the other an underground cemetery for the many.

Lager *vs.* Ale

Lagers look clear and taste crisp.

LAGER

Ales look hazy and taste rich.

ALE

The Fine Print

Lagers are brewed slowly and at cold temperatures using one sort of yeast. Ales are brewed quickly and at warm temperatures using another. Virtually all beers fall into one category or the other.

Though their key distinction lies in the type of yeast used, the brewing temperature makes a big difference too: Inhibiting the yeast's activity during fermentation, the chilled environment of lagers produces a cleaner-drinking finish, while the warmer, more frenzied atmosphere in which ale yeast flourishes creates a more fully flavored brew. But this is just a general rule, as beer wizards can pull all kinds of tricks.

Classic lagers include pilsners and other pale lagers—think Budweiser, Heineken, or Corona—while ales come in a wide variety of forms, from IPAs and wheat beers to brown ales, porters, and stouts. Note that while lagers can be dark in color (as with dunkels and bocks), they are less common than their golden-yellow counterparts. Ales, meanwhile, are variously colored, and need not be hazy or opaque, though they tend to be when compared to lagers.

In short, lagers are your classic go-to for a crisp, refreshing, and easy-drinking beer, while ales open up a broad spectrum of complex flavors and aromas, with profiles ranging from sweet and fruity to spicy and bitter.

Lattice *vs.* Trellis

Lattices are for dividing space and are diamond- or square-shaped.

LATTICE

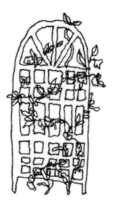

Trellises are for growing plants and come in a variety of patterns.

TRELLIS

Lattices double as trellises. Trellises are often lattice-shaped.

Crossing the Line

Lattices serve a variety of purposes, from shaping a space to establishing privacy to improving airflow where previously there was a solid wall. More broadly, the term refers to crisscrossing diamond- or square-shaped patterns wherever they may be found, as for example on top of pies.

Oxford English Dictionary (OED) vs. Oxford Dictionary of English (ODE)

OXFORD ENGLISH DICTIONARY (OED)

OXFORD DICTIONARY OF ENGLISH (ODE)

The *OED* is a multi-volume record of the history of the English language.

The *ODE* is a single-volume dictionary of English as it is currently used.

Both are published by Oxford University Press (OUP).

USAGE NOTE

People often say that they looked it up in the *OED* when they probably just mean the *ODE*—unless, of course, they own all twenty volumes of the *OED* and plan to tell you how the word (which may be obsolete) has been used in every century since it was first recorded.

Gala *vs.* Ball

GALA

A gala is a large, upscale social event.

BALL

A ball is a large, upscale social event with dancing.

JPEG *vs.* PNG

JPEGs take up less storage space and are good for photographs that would otherwise be hefty.

JPEG

PNGs preserve resolution and are good for simple graphics that aren't that big to begin with.

PNG

File Types

Saving an image as a JPEG (or JPG) is good for reducing its file size, especially in the case of photographs or paintings whose complexity would otherwise cause it to take up more storage space, slow down web page load times, etc. JPEG image compression works by averaging out (and deleting) color differences, and depending on the degree of compression, loss of image fidelity can range from imperceptible to unignorable.

LOW-RES JPEG

Saving an image as a PNG is good for keeping your images clean and sharp, especially in the case of simple, high-contrast digital graphics that aren't that big to begin with: icons, line drawings, text-based images, etc. PNG image compression works by eliminating redundant file data and arranging what's left more efficiently. Maintaining original image quality, this compression style is considered "lossless" (as opposed to the "lossy" approach of the JPEG file format). As you might expect, however, PNG compression doesn't shrink the file quite as much.

Unlike JPEGs, PNGs also support transparent backgrounds, making it great for adding graphics to layouts without bringing a glaring white box along with it.

Joint *vs.* Spliff

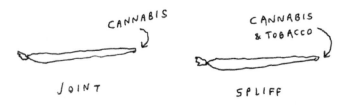

JOINT

Joints contain nothing but cannabis.

SPLIFF

Spliffs sprinkle in a little tobacco.

ONE MORE

Like joints, blunts are pure cannabis on the inside—only they're rolled in tobacco paper (blunt wraps) or hollowed-out cigars, giving them a different taste and a slower burn.

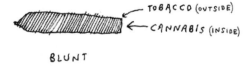

BLUNT

Missile *vs.* Torpedo

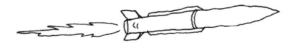

MISSILE

Missiles are rocket-powered
weapons that fly through the air.

TORPEDO

Torpedoes are propeller-powered
weapons that cruise underwater.

Technically, torpedoes are a type of missile, but when
people think of missiles, they tend to picture those at top.

Lute *vs.* Lyre

Lutes are long-necked and pear-shaped. Popular in Renaissance and Baroque Europe.

LUTE

Lyres are U-shaped and flat-backed. Popular in ancient Greece and Rome.

LYRE

Because of their fingerboards, lutes let you modulate pitch while playing, making them frankly the better instrument.

String Theory

The word lute may also be used more broadly to designate the family of necked-and-stringed instruments as a whole: Ouds, pipas, and other variants throughout the world, for instance, can all be classified as lutes.

Conversely, the word lyre may be used more narrowly to refer to just *one* of many such U-shaped instruments from Greece and Asia Minor, other examples being the kithara, the barbiton, and the phorminx. Because of how their strings are suspended, these lyre-family instruments are sometimes classified as "yoke lutes." So much for keeping them separate.

Strategy *vs.* Tactics

A strategy is a general approach in pursuit of a goal. A tactic is a specific action taken to help pull it off.

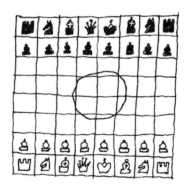

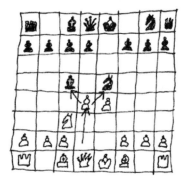

STRATEGY   TACTICS

EXAMPLE

Controlling the center of the chessboard is a strategy. Forking enemy pieces to do so is a tactic.

Picking a Lane

Whether in war, politics, business, or games, strategy refers to the formation of an overarching approach—to the exclusion of others—in pursuit of victory or success. Tactics, by contrast, refers to the grab bag of maneuvers called for by your particular strategy such that they work together rather than at cross-purposes. One tends to be set in advance by the leadership, the other to be deployed on the fly by those on the ground.

"Strategy is a pattern in a stream of decisions."
—Henry Mintzberg

Rational *vs.* Reasonable

To be rational is to be logical.

Rational explanation

RATIONAL

To be reasonable is to be sensible.

Reasonable request

REASONABLE

One is about thinking carefully in the abstract.
The other is about being fair or balanced in real life.

The Voice(s) of Reason

R ationality lets us pursue a single train of thought—sometimes to the point of tunnel vision. Reasonableness exposes our myopia to a broader, if blurrier, view.

> *Your argument that humans should*
> *stop procreating is perfectly rational.*
> *It's also totally unreasonable.*

Irony *vs.* Sarcasm

Irony is when you say one thing but mean another.

So is sarcasm, only what you mean is insulting.

Lounging on the beach:
"It's a tough life."

After someone trips:
"Smooth move."

The Fine Print

Irony is when your intended meaning differs from, or is even opposed to, what you actually say, a rhetorical device that can be put to humorous or belittling effect. When the latter, it's called sarcasm.

Irony

Sarcasm

Breathless after a marathon:
"Piece of cake."

After a friend screws up:
"Good going, Einstein."

Not all examples are so obvious, however, as the line separating humor from bite can sometimes be hard to draw. "The sergeant's a ray of sunshine," for instance, may be considered funny or disparaging, ironic or sarcastic, depending on whether it's a welcome observation or an against-the-grain remark—whether it's said with a friendly wink or in a mocking tone of voice.

Though many authorities (among them H. W. Fowler, Merriam-Webster, and the *OED*) claim that irony and sarcasm can exist independently of one another, I cannot think of a single sarcastic statement that I would not also call ironic, suggesting (at least to me) that sarcasm is more a weaponized subcategory of irony than anything distinct.

Note, finally, that only *verbal* irony is here under consideration—the one type of irony with which sarcasm is confused. For other types (dramatic, situational), see page 126.

Doula *vs.* Midwife

Doulas offer guidance and emotional support.

DOULA

Midwives help physically deliver the baby.

MIDWIFE

They are not mutually exclusive.

Kinds of Care

Doulas are nonmedical workers who provide information, guidance, and emotional and physical comfort before, during, and after childbirth. Though no certification is required for doulas in the US or the UK, many doulas complete some form of training.

Midwives help deliver babies and provide obstetrical support before, during, and after childbirth to ensure the physical health of both mother and child. Midwives fall roughly into two categories: those whose training in midwifery is preceded by a nursing degree (nurse-midwives) and those whose training isn't (direct entry).

Farm *vs.* Ranch

FARM

Farms grow crops and/or rear animals.

RANCH

Ranches just rear animals, and only the big grazing ones.

If you grow wheat or raise chickens, you're a farmer. If you herd cattle, sheep, or goats on open pastures, you're a rancher—maybe even a cowboy.

Hue *vs.* Tint *vs.* Shade *vs.* Tone

Hues are colors. Tints add white to make them lighter. Shades add black to make them darker. Tones add gray to make them worse.

Shades of Meaning

Hue refers to any identifiable color on the color wheel—red, orange, yellow, etc.—or anything in between those colors—red-orange, yellow-green, etc.—regardless of that color's lightness or intensity. Whether it's a light blue, dark blue, intense blue, or muted blue, the hue is the same in each case—blue.

Tints and shades, by contrast, tweak a particular hue's lightness (or value) by adding variable amounts of white and black, respectively. Pink is a tint of red, for instance, while brown, believe it or not, is a shade of orange—neither of these generally being considered pure hues but, like pale green or midnight blue, only lighter or darker modifications thereof.

Tones, finally, alter a hue's intensity (or chroma) by adding greater or lesser amounts of gray, which, as a blend of white and black, means you're effectively tinting and shading at the same time. The result is a duller, more muted version of the original, fully chromatic hue. Though tones seem like a boring choice, sometimes colors are too intense and you need to, well, tone it down a bit.

Value *vs.* Chroma

Color theory is a bottomless, though kaleidoscopic pit, with many competing and complementary systems. Drawing on Munsell's tripartite model of hue, value, and chroma, value generally refers to our perception of a color's relative lightness or darkness, whereas chroma broadly refers to a color's intensity or lack thereof. Note that a color may raise or lower its value yet hold on to most of its chroma and vice versa, though there is a general tendency of one to affect the other.

Pier *vs.* Quay *vs.* Wharf

PIER

Piers jut out from the shoreline.

QUAY

Quays run parallel to it.

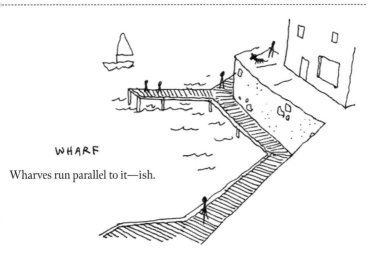

WHARF

Wharves run parallel to it—ish.

Altered Shores

Piers are typically raised high on piles, as shown, but the term may refer to solid land extensions, too. Unlike wharves and quays, which are designed to facilitate docking, some "pleasure piers" function simply as promenades. Whatever their shape or function, piers run perpendicular to the shoreline.

The terms quay and wharf are used somewhat interchangeably—especially in the US, where quay is less common—yet quays tend to refer to solid (stone or cement) modifications of the shoreline, wharves to structures raised on piles that go beyond it. As distinct constructions, wharves tend to be irregular in shape, often with a base running parallel to the shoreline made jagged by piers and boxy protrusions as needed.

Dock, finally, is an umbrella term for any structure where boats or ships can, as the name suggests, dock. In the UK, however, dock refers to the water rather than the land, which honestly makes more sense: It's where the boat docks.

Ponzi Scheme *vs.* Pyramid Schem[e]

PONZI SCHEME

Ponzi schemes pay past investors with future investments, skimming off the top all the while.

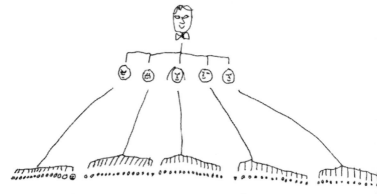

PYRAMID SCHEME

Pyramid schemes recruit and charge members for permission to recruit and charge members, again skimming off the top.

One robs Peter to pay Paul.
The other charges Peter for permission to charge Paul.

Two Swindles

Ponzi schemes are fake investment opportunities: Instead of investing in an actual entity, investors are paid "returns" consisting of money taken from those who come after them, usually at a high rate in order to help spread the word and keep the cycle going. Eventually, however, the rate of investment slows, returns start to thin out, and the schemer who has been skimming off the top the whole time pulls the cord on the whole thing and makes off with everyone's principal, too.

Pyramid schemes aren't fake investment opportunities so much as shady *business* opportunities: Rather than passively invest in the hope of a return, you pay a membership fee for the right to actively sell that business's product and, more importantly, to recruit more members and keep a percentage of their buy-in fee. In the end, though, the lion's share goes to the schemer at the top, and most members never even recoup their original membership costs, let alone make a profit.

ADVANCED DISTINCTION

Multi-Level Marketing (MLM)

Multi-level marketing companies resemble pyramid schemes but are in fact legal, principally because member earnings derive less from recruiting others than from actually selling the product. Still, many pyramid schemes will pose as legitimate MLMs, making it hard to distinguish between the two.

Ristorante *vs.* Trattoria *vs.* Osteria

RISTORANTE

Ristorantes are formal.

TRATTORIA

Trattorias are casual.

OSTERIA

Osterias are *very* casual.

Out for Dinner

A ristorante is a full-service Italian restaurant: professional staff, sophisticated atmosphere, refined cuisine, elevated prices.

A trattoria is a smaller, more casual Italian restaurant: family-run, relaxed environment, regional menu, moderate prices.

An osteria is a smaller, *much* more casual Italian restaurant: basic furnishings, economy pricing, and just one or two rotating items on the board—basically, whatever they picked up from the market.

WORDS REPURPOSED

Despite the humble meanings of *trattoria* and *osteria*, wily restaurateurs will often borrow these terms for their exotic twang, then charge you through the nose for it. Same goes for *bistro*, which originally denoted a smaller, more casual version of the French *restaurant*.

> *"... we lunched with Philip in a restaurant*
> *which though small was not a mere bistro."*
>
> —Rebecca West, *Black Lamb and Grey Falcon:*
> *A Journey Through Yugoslavia*

Clementine *vs.* Tangerine *vs.* Mandarin

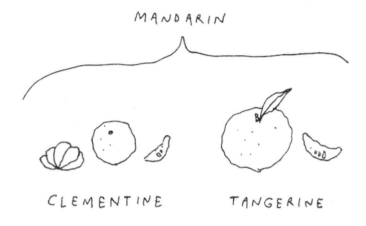

Clementines are light orange, small, seedless, and sweet, while tangerines are deep orange, larger, seeded, and tart. Generally speaking, anyway.

Mandarin is an umbrella term referring to these and other diminutive oranges.

MNEMONIC

Clementines are tiny.
Tangerines are tangy.
Mandarins are many.

Fruit Sex

Owing to the wide variety of hybrids, citrus taxonomy is a bit of a mess. Clementines and tangerines tend to be classed as mandarins, for instance, yet strictly speaking they are crossbred descendants of the mandarin and the pomelo—as are, ultimately, the grapefruit and even the orange, each with their own variants and cultivars. In short, citrus fruits are less a rigid typology than an orgiastic free-for-all where cousins, parents, and children continue to form new varieties, all ultimately descending from a few ancestral species.

Jargon *vs.* Slang

Jargon is language you don't understand because it's specific to a particular field of knowledge.

Slang is language you don't understand because it's specific to a particular subculture.

Medical jargon

Internet slang

> *"... a mix of quasi-military jargon, street slang, rough epithets, and a fair bit of gallows humor—in other words, cop-speak."*
>
> —Graham Rayman, *The Village Voice*, 2010

Languages Within Language

At its best, jargon consists of specialized terms and expressions for which there is no easy equivalent in everyday language, spoken among individuals with experience in the same field: *affidavit, megahertz, ileoanal anastomosis*. Yet jargon can also confuse, exclude, and/or annoy outsiders, whether it's spoken accidentally through force of habit or in an ill-judged attempt to impress. Even worse, jargon can be used to dodge or downplay the truth, most notoriously in corporate and political contexts, where a slew of firings is called destaffing and the bombing defenseless villages, as George Orwell pointed out, is rebranded as pacification.

Slang, by contrast, has less to do with articulating a field of knowledge than a field of *experience*: the interests, attitudes, and perspectives of teens, punks, African Americans, LGBTQ+ communities, or indeed any sociocultural group with a shared ethos, especially those on the margins of, or which have been marginalized *by*, mainstream culture: *cool, ghost, shook, sus, dank*. Slang is a powerful counterforce in language and in life—one able to crystallize new experiences and attitudes, bond groups together through shared vocabulary, and destabilize status quo modes of speech.

Note, however, that while jargon comes across as *more* formal than everyday language, slang comes across as less so: Imparting a shared worldview, slang tends to feel familiar.

Stock *vs.* Bond

Stocks represent something you own: a piece of a company whose value in the market can skyrocket, tank, or do anything in between.

Bonds represent something you *loan*: a piece of debt issued by a company or government that they are obligated to repay at a set interest rate.

In short: With stocks, you're buying; with bonds, you're lending. Also: Stocks are riskier than bonds, but carry the appeal of a higher reward.

A Few More Frankly Unintuitive Financial Terms

- **EQUITY.** Though the word has other meanings, in the world of finance, equity refers to the dollar value of any asset you own less whatever debts you may have on it. If your car is worth $30K, for instance, but you still owe $20K in financing payments, you have $10K in equity on that car. By paying off your mortgage, the amount of equity you have in your home steadily goes up. Stocks, or "equities" as they're sometimes called, are no different: They indicate the value of your ownership stake in a company, minus that company's liabilities. Note that one such liability is the debt owed to bondholders: As lenders rather than owners, they are paid first in the event that a company goes under.

- **SECURITY.** Another word with a distinct meaning in finance, a security is roughly any financial asset that you can buy, sell, or trade. Effectively an umbrella category, securities come in two two major varieties—equity securities (stocks) and debt securities (bonds)—alongside a few other financial concoctions like options and derivatives.

Stock *vs.* Broth

STOCK

Stock is made by simmering bones and joints in water for long periods of time. It tends to be unseasoned.

BROTH

Broth is made by simmering meat or fish in water for shorter periods of time. It is almost always seasoned.

Both tend to involve vegetables.

The Fine Print

Because of the collagen in the bones and other skeletal bits, stock tends to be gelatinous, making it a good thickener for stews, sauces, and gravies. And because stock tends to be unseasoned, it provides a more neutral base for whatever it is you're making.

Stock *vs.* Broth, *cont.*

Broth, meanwhile, is thinner and saltier, making it both a good flavoring agent and a source of liquid volume in soups, stews, etc. Still, in many if not most dishes, you can substitute one for the other; just be mindful of the level of seasoning going in.

As for *veggie* stocks and broths, since vegetables don't have any collagen, the two are virtually identical—although, as above, the term broth may mean there's more salt.

MORE IN THE POT

Admittedly, stocks may add meat, fish, etc., while broths may add bones, joints, etc., but these additions are optional.

Bone broth is, as you might guess, made primarily from bones, so strictly speaking it's more of a stock. The things we do for alliteration.

Harbor *vs.* Port *vs.* Marina

Harbors are enclosed bodies of water whose minimal wind and waves allow ships to moor or anchor safely.

Ports are harbors designed to handle commercial-scale loading and unloading.

Marinas are harbors designed for yachts and smaller watercraft.

Thicket *vs.* Grove

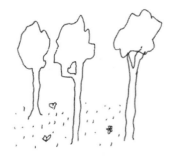

THICKET

GROVE

Thickets have underbrush.

Groves don't.

ADVANCED DISTINCTION

ORCHARD

A deliberately planted rather than naturally occurring grove.

The Fine Print

Groves are nice to walk through; so much so, in fact, that some cultures hold them sacred. Thickets are uniformly unenjoyable to walk through.

Despite their name, orange groves are as deliberate as apple orchards—orange orchard is just kind of hard to say.

Grammar *vs.* Syntax

Grammar refers to the rules that govern language in general.

Syntax refers to the rules that govern sentences in particular.

The Fine Print

Grammar is an umbrella term for the various structures that make up a language and govern its use, covering everything from the identification of different parts of speech (noun, verb, adjective, etc.) to the rules governing individual word inflection (by tense, case, number, etc.). According to some, grammar even encompasses principles of linguistic sound (phonology) and meaning (semantics).

Syntax is a subfield of grammar. Specifically, syntax refers to the rules governing sentence structure and describes how words may be clustered and arranged to form complete sentences. In short, syntax is about word order, or where everything *goes*. Exposing a sentence's syntax by breaking it down into its constituent parts is known as "parsing."

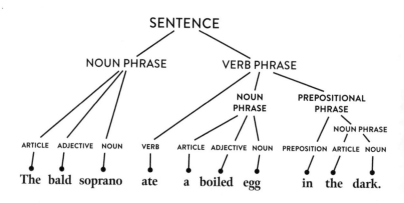

Among linguists, syntax is frequently contrasted with morphology, the branch of grammar concerning individual words, stems, and their modifications (*thief thieves*). Put differently, morphology concerns *word* structure, while syntax concerns *sentence* structure, or the meaningful arrangement of multiple words. Together, syntax and morphology make up the lion's share of grammar.

Syntax Unbound

Famously, Noam Chomsky used the sentence "Colorless green ideas sleep furiously" to expose the difference between syntax and semantics: Though semantically meaningless—it has no real sense or reference—it is syntactically sound. "Furiously sleep ideas green colorless," by contrast, is neither.

Hay *vs.* Straw

Hay is the greenish stuff that farm animals eat.

HAY

Straw is the yellowish stuff that farm animals sleep on.

STRAW

The Fine Print

Hay refers to the cuttings of certain grasses or plants (e.g., alfalfa, orchard grass) that have been grown and harvested for the express purpose of feeding livestock.

Straw, by contrast, refers to the dried yellow stalks of cereal plants (wheat, barley, oat) left over after the edible grain of the plant has been removed. A by-product of harvesting, in other words, straw is used for everything from animal bedding to roof thatching, plant mulching to hat weaving.

Unlike hay, straw is hollow. Just like the ones we drink through. Straw is also cheap—probably why they use it on hayrides.

4/4 Time *vs.* 2/2 Time

4/4 TIME

4/4 time is good for most music.

2/2 TIME

2/2 time is good for fast music.

A Musical Riddle

For any basic time signature, the top number tells you how many beats are in a bar, while the bottom number tells you the value of each beat.

In 4/4 time, for instance, every bar is made up of four beats, with a quarter note counting as a single beat. In 2/2 time, by contrast, each bar has only two beats, with a half note counting as a single beat.

But then you might be wondering: *Don't these two time signatures amount to the same thing?* Four quarter notes and two half notes are equal in value, after all, and you can use either note in either time signature. So what gives?

While mathematically 4/4 and 2/2 are identical, musically they are not. In fact, they're different in two ways: (1) their typical stress pattern, and (2) their readability at high speeds.

Starting with their stress pattern, it's important to remember that in 4/4 time, the top number tells us to count four beats per bar *regardless of how many notes there are*, while in 2/2 time it's the same idea: two main beats regardless of the number of notes.

While that may not seem like such a big deal, the higher-beat four-count gives musicians room to explore a wider range of intensities along the way, frequently leading them to stress their beats according to a "strong-weak-medium-weak" accent structure (*one*-two-three-four, *one*-two-three-four). Try counting to four a few times and you may find yourself falling into this stress pattern.

Old MacDonald / had a farm, / ee-ei ee-ei / oh

In 2/2 time, however, the two-count tends to encourage only two stress options: strong and weak. A bit more black and white, 2/2 tends to be the time signature of choice for "Left, right!"-style military marches and punchier music more broadly, whether light and bouncy or grand and stately. *One*-two, *one*-two . . .

But all that has to do with the top number (beats per bar), making what is true of 2/2 equally true of 2/4 or any 2/*n*: the two-count encourages a more binary stress pattern.

As for the *value* of each beat (the bottom number), doubling the length of what's measured from a quarter note (/4) to a half note (/2) allows composers to write faster pieces of music without clogging up their pages with a bunch of busy-looking thirty-second and sixty-fourth notes, which is otherwise what you'd have to do (assuming the same number of beats per minute, say, quarter notes or half notes at 60 bpm).

The same quick piece of music in 4/4 time and 2/2 time.

Again, that may not seem like a big deal, but long bars full of complex notes, which is what fast music looks like in 4/4, is harder for musicians to read, while shorter bars with simpler notes, which is what fast music looks like in 2/2, is comparatively easy.

Incidentally, 4/4 time is sometimes referred to as common time and indicated by a **C**, while 2/2 time is sometimes called cut time (or alla breve) and indicated with a **¢**. It "cuts" 4/4 time in half.

Common time is the prevailing time signature of pop, rock, hip-hop, classical, and Western music more broadly.

Verbal Irony *vs.* Dramatic Irony

Verbal irony is when you say one thing but mean another.

Dramatic irony is when *they* say one thing but it means more than they realize.

During a fire drill:
"Ah, peace and quiet."

Piano falling overhead:
"I love music, don't you?"

Where Incongruities Arise

Verbal irony is a rhetorical device in which the speaker conveys their meaning by stating the opposite, or at least something quite different, and letting the context do the work of clarifying what they mean. An indirect use of language, verbal irony lets you say what you want to say without saying it.

Dramatic irony is a literary device in which the audience or reader knows more about what's happening than the characters themselves, such that the character says something, or does something, that has implications they don't realize. The effect may be suspenseful (*Don't go in there!*), comic (*Don't go in there, you idiot!*), or tragic (*Don't drink that poison, Romeo!*). The last of these, naturally, is also called "tragic irony."

What both types of irony have in common is an incongruity between appearance and reality—whether between what one says and what one means, or between what a character thinks is the case and what *is* the case. Yet while verbal irony is deliberate, dramatic irony is unwitting (at least on the part of the speaker), and while the former is verbal, the latter may be verbal or behavioral.

Ironic Subtypes

- **SOCRATIC IRONY:** A type of verbal irony in which the speaker feigns ignorance to force their opponent to explain themselves, especially when the latter won't be able to do a good job: *I see! So justice amounts to hurting your enemies ... which means that hurting people is a good thing?* Socrates uses it in most of Plato's dialogues and it's super annoying.

- **STRUCTURAL IRONY:** Another application of verbal irony where not just one sentence but an entire piece is opposed to the author's true meaning, as in Jonathan Swift's essay "A Modest Proposal": "I have been assured by a very knowing American of my acquaintance in London, that a young healthy child well nursed is at a year old a most delicious, nourishing, and wholesome food, whether stewed, roasted, baked, or boiled ..." In other words, satire.

- **SITUATIONAL IRONY:** Alongside verbal and dramatic, a third category of irony in which the nature or outcome of a situation is the diametric opposite of what was expected or desired—a so-called twist of fate. It's the kind of irony we most often use to describe real-life events, as when the fire station burns down or you barber has a bad haircut.

"So justice, according to you and Homer and Simonides, seems to be a kind of stealing ... Isn't that what you meant?"

"No, by Zeus," he replied ...

—Plato, *The Republic*, book I, 334*

On the difference between verbal irony and sarcasm, see page 96.

* Plato, *Plato in Twelve Volumes*, vols. 5 & 6, trans. Paul Shorey (Cambridge, MA: Harvard University Press, 1969).

Deadlift *vs.* Romanian Deadlift

In a conventional deadlift, you extend all the way to the ground.

DEADLIFT

In a Romanian deadlift, you don't.

ROMANIAN
DEADLIFT

A Shift in Position

The Romanian deadlift's narrower range of motion means you don't have to bend your knees as much, which in turn isolates the hamstrings and glutes better—although it also leaves out your quads so you can't lift as much. In short, RDLs are good for targeting certain muscles, while conventional deadlifts are good for all-around strength.

Gully *vs.* Ravine *vs.* Gorge *vs.* Canyon

GULLY

RAVINE

Gullies are small. Canyons are huge. Ravines and gorges are somewhere in the middle, with gorges tending to be the steeper and rockier of the two. Basically, gorges are smaller canyons.

All four trenches are formed by running water (active or otherwise) carving progressively bigger swaths out of the earth.

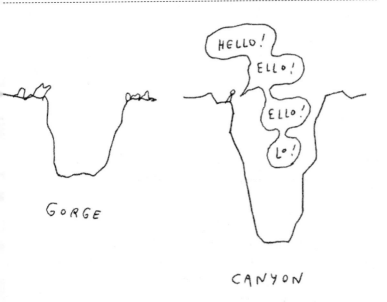

GORGE

CANYON

Civil Law *vs.* Common Law

Civil law is based on statutes written by lawmakers.

Common law is based on precedents set in court.

In one system, judges apply the law.
In the other, they continuously shape it.

The Fine Print

The civil law system is arguably closer to one's intuitive sense of the law: Statutes are enacted by the legislature and collected into a code, then applied by judges to the facts of the case.

The common law system, by contrast, refers to a living body of court decisions known as case law, whereby past judicial rulings set precedents for similar cases in the future. Where existing case law is deemed inapplicable to the case at hand, judges have the power to set a new precedent. Common law judges also tend to play a more referee-like role in court, leaving the establishing of facts and witness examinations to the prosecution and defense; civil law judges, by comparison, are more hands-on.

Most nations in Europe, Latin America, and East Asia have a civil law system. The US, the UK, and most Commonwealth countries have a common law one.

Overstating the Case

It is worth noting, however, that statutes exist in common law countries, too, meaning that case law doesn't *replace* statue law in those countries so much as supplement it—it fills in the gaps.

Muddying the difference still more, civil law countries will nevertheless look to legal precedent, if not as binding (as in the case of common law countries), then at least as informative.

In short, despite these systems' abstract differences, both sets of nations effectively rely on a mixed legal system wherein judicial precedent is called in (with greater or lesser force) to address issues not covered by statutes.

Street *vs.* Boulevard *vs.* Avenue *vs.* Road

| Streets are urban. | Boulevards are wide. | Avenues are boulevardish. | All of them are roads. |

The Fine Print

Boulevards are broad, and are often adorned with a tree-lined median or flanks. The most extravagant of the bunch, they're usually long and straight, too: big arterial thoroughfares connecting different parts of the city.

Streets, by contrast, *are* the city: narrower stretches lined with buildings, shops, and homes—the places where we live and work. If boulevards are mighty thoroughfares, streets are their last-mile veins and capillaries.

Avenues are boulevard wannabes. Often wider than streets and with a higher speed limit to match, avenues may even sport a median or lapels, or terminate at a large monument or park—as their name, which derives from the French verb meaning "to approach," suggests. But just as often, any old street will put on airs and go by the name avenue, maybe because it's a particularly nice one, or simply to mix it up, or perhaps because the planner in charge didn't like the verbal traffic jam that arises when you try to say "Fisk Street." In many US cities (NYC, Chicago, Denver, and Memphis, to name a few), avenues are simply roads that run perpendicular to streets. Avenues, in short, are a shifty bunch.

Road, finally, is an umbrella term, albeit one with a rural connotation that, as cities expand and swallow up more and more of them, is increasingly hard to hear.

More Roads

- *Drives* are winding, scenic, private, or all of the above.
- *Crescents* are circular, semicircular, or crescent-shaped.
- *Places* are simple dead ends.
- *Courts* are dead ends that terminate in an open circle (i.e., a cul-de-sac).

Pasture *vs.* Meadow

PASTURE

A pasture is an open grassy area for livestock to graze on.

MEADOW

A meadow is an open grassy area left to grow for later mowing and haying: animal fodder for the offseason.

By extension, the term meadow may refer to untamed grassy areas more broadly—think fields with pretty wildflowers.

Parody *vs.* Satire

Parody is the imitation of a work of art or general style for comedic effect.

Satire is parody with intent to criticize social or political vice in the real world.

A Star Wars *parody*

A satire on American politics

Parody tends to be light and amusing.
Satire's usually more abrasive.

Shades of Scorn

Satires have more critical bite, but parodies aren't harmless either. What a parody mimics, and thereby mocks, are the tropes and sensibilities of a certain style, especially as they approach cliché. When those crime dramas and rom-coms start to feel formulaic, parody swoops in and skewers them via exaggeration and inversion.

Still, satire tends to cut deeper, attacking as it does real-life political figures, religious groups, social attitudes, etc. For satire, importantly, the point isn't the critique of style but of *substance*, showcasing deplorable beliefs and behaviors to expose their immorality. Often the style imitated isn't even the primary target, but only a pretext to criticize something else: *Gulliver's Travels* parodies travel literature, but satirizes human folly. *Animal Farm* parodies children's fables, but satirizes Stalinism.

PARODIES
(AND THEIR TARGETS)

- *Austin Powers* (James Bond)
- *Scary Movie* (horror movies)
- *Don Quixote* (chivalric romance)
- *Spaceballs* (Star Wars)
- *Galaxy Quest* (Star Trek)
- Shakespeare's Sonnet 130 (love poetry)
- *This Is Spinal Tap* (music documentaries)

SATIRES
(AND THEIR TARGETS)

- *The Daily Show* (politics and society)
- *The Office* (corporate culture)
- "A Modest Proposal" (neglect of the poor)
- *Dr. Strangelove* (nuclear war strategy)
- *Animal Farm* (Stalinism)
- *Brave New World* (technocracy)
- *Saturday Night Live* (politics and society)

EST *vs.* EDT *vs.* ET

EST

EDT

ET

EST, or Eastern Standard Time, is 5 hours behind Coordinated Universal Time (UTC) in Greenwich. EST is the default time in its region, observed in the fall and winter.*

EDT, or Eastern Daylight Time, is 4 hours behind UTC, a 1-hour advance from EST due to daylight saving time. It's the modified time in the region, in effect during spring and summer.

ET, or Eastern Time, is ambiguous. When in doubt, use it to mean "whichever one we're in now."

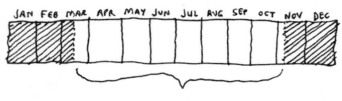

DAYLIGHT SAVING TIME

* Readers will hopefully forgive me for choosing my own time zone to illustrate the difference. In most other regions of North America and Europe, the principle is the same, although less so elsewhere. For further discussion, see page 191.

The Quest for Light

Despite being called "standard," EST is quite a bit shorter than its daylight saving counterpart. At least that's the case in North America, where EST runs from the first Sunday of November to the second Sunday of March—a little over four months. EDT, by contrast, covers the longer, warmer remainder of the year, where pushing our clocks forward an hour effectively shifts more of that glorious summer sunlight to the evening when we can properly enjoy it. No sense sleeping through it, after all.

But tinkering with our clocks twice a year is a surprisingly controversial practice—and, globally, a shrinking one. While vast swaths of Africa, Asia, and Latin America once embraced a two-time system, nowadays few countries in those regions do. And while it's still practiced in most of North America and Europe, the EU was on the brink of abandoning it in 2021 when something more important came along (COVID-19) and made them defer. There's a big anti-tinker lobby in the US, too.

Advocates of alternating between standard and daylight saving time claim that it saves energy, reduces crime, and promotes outdoor evening activity (both physical and economic), while detractors argue that it screws up our sleep cycles, triggers car crashes and heart attacks, wastes more energy than it conserves, and is generally confusing and annoying—especially when coordinating between regions that change their clocks at different times of the year. They have a point, there.

Modernity *vs.* Modernism

MODERNITY

Modernity is a historical period.

MODERNISM

Modernism is a cultural movement.

The Fine Print

Modernity refers to the period roughly spanning the mid-1400s to the mid-1900s, though some historians start later or extend it to the present day. Whatever your dates, the idea is that modernity generally refers to the post-medieval world—a world that gradually became more rational, urban, industrial, individualistic, secular, capitalist, and liberal. What follows modernity is sometimes called the contemporary period, though in lay contexts both modern and contemporary roughly mean nowadays as opposed to the past, or up-to-date as opposed to old-fashioned.

Modernism, by contrast, is a literary, artistic, and philosophical movement that was in vogue from roughly the 1890s to the 1940s. Modernist works are characterized by a fascination with novelty and the desire to break with the past; a fragmented sense of time and space; a preference for creativity over imitation; and formal experimentation. Notable modernists include Virginia Woolf (stream-of-consciousness novels), Pablo Picasso (cubism), Arnold Schoenberg (twelve-tone technique), and Ludwig Mies van der Rohe (International Style architecture).

Fusilli *vs.* Rotini

FUSILLI

Fusilli refers to corkscrew pasta, whether spun by hand or extruded through a machine.

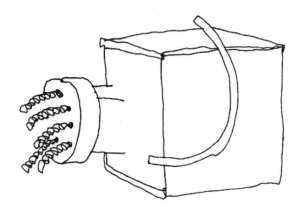

FUSILLI / ROTINI

Rotini is a chiefly North American term for the same noodle, though it tends to suggest the boxed variety (fusilli is a bit either/or). The term is also less common in culinary circles, where fusilli remains the word of choice.

A False Distinction

A few writers online claim that fusilli is spun by hand and loosely coiled, while rotini is machine extruded and tightly wound. But boxed, tightly wound pasta by De Cecco and Garofalo labeled "fusilli" suggests otherwise, reducing what might've been a material difference to a largely regional one.

Mesa *vs.* Butte

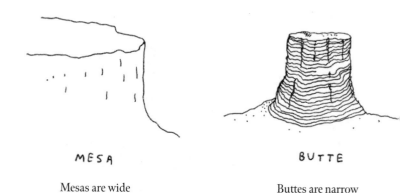

MESA

BUTTE

Mesas are wide
flat-topped hills.

Buttes are narrow
flat-topped hills.

One turns into the other via erosion.

The Fine Print

According to *National Geographic*, mesas are wider than they are tall, while buttes are taller than they are wide—a handy rule of thumb. *Mesa* also means "table" in Spanish, so it's a fitting name for something wide and flat. The debris that piles up around the base of mesas and buttes, finally, is called scree, also known as talus.

Phrase *vs.* Clause

PHRASE

My very lazy cat *(noun phrase)*
dozed on the couch *(verb phrase)*
very lazy *(adjectival phrase)*
on the couch *(prepositional phrase)*

Phrases are groups of words defined by a single part of speech, whether noun, verb, adjective, etc. Thus they can never have both a subject (noun) and a verb, which are needed to form a complete sentence.

CLAUSE

While I prepared breakfast,
(dependent clause)
my cat dozed on the couch
(independent clause)

Clauses are groups of words with subject-verb pairings. They can either be a complete sentence (independent clause) or attached to one (dependent clause).

Building Sentences

Phrases are like Lego blocks: They can be combined in a variety of ways to create a finished product, but are never a finished product on their own.

Clauses are like modular homes: They may be suitable on their own, or tacked on to one that is.

Wicker *vs.* Rattan

WICKER

Wicker is the style.

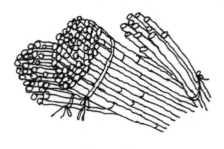

RATTAN

Rattan is the material.

The Fine Print

Wicker is a style of furniture-making and basketry in which pliable plant materials are woven or braided into shape.

Rattan refers to a class of palm vines commonly used in the fabrication of wicker. Other popular materials include willow, bamboo, and, of course, plastic.

When you peel off the bark from rattan stems, finally, you get cane—a flatter, more delicate material commonly found along the sides, backs, and seats of chairs in an octagonal pattern called cane webbing.

Flotsam *vs.* Jetsam

FLOTSAM

Flotsam is debris that spills out from a shipwreck of its own accord.

JETSAM

Jetsam is debris that's deliberately thrown overboard—namely, in order to prevent a shipwreck.

Rough Seas

According to maritime law, if you find flotsam, it may be claimed by its original owner, but if you find jetsam, it's yours. Technically, the owner gave it away.

MNEMONIC

Flotsam floats away.
Jetsam is jettisoned.

Crumble *vs.* Crisp *vs.* Cobbler

CRUMBLE

Crumbles are baked fruit dishes topped with a mixture of flour, butter, and sugar.

CRISP

Crisps are baked fruit dishes topped with a mixture of flour, butter, sugar, and *oats*.

COBBLER

Cobblers, finally, are baked fruit dishes topped with biscuits, cookie dough, cake batter, or the like—something with baking powder to give it volume.

It's All in the Name

Crumbles are crumbly because of the butter-flour-sugar mixture (streusel). Crisps are crispy because of the added oats. Cobblers, finally, are cobblery because the dough tends to form clumps resembling cobblestones.

Hansom *vs.* Barouche *vs.* Stagecoach *vs.* Troika

HANSOM

Hansoms are one-horsed, two-wheeled, nimble little cabs that can seat up to two passengers, with the driver at the back.

BAROUCHE

Barouches are two-horsed, four-wheeled, stately private carriages that can seat up to four, with the driver up front.

STAGECOACH

Stagecoaches are four-horsed, four-wheeled, enclosed public vehicles. They follow scheduled routes and can seat six or more.

TROIKA

Troikas, finally, are sleighs drawn by three horses harnessed abreast. A symbol of Russian culture, troikas move really fast.

GENERAL TERMS

- *Cab* suggests that the vehicle is for hire.
- *Coach* suggests that the vehicle is enclosed.
- *Carriage* suggests that the vehicle is privately owned.

More Horse-Drawn Vehicles

- **FOUR-IN-HAND:** Any four-horse carriage with a single driver, especially those used in racing.
- **HORSE AND BUGGY:** Any light, simple, partly or fully enclosed two-seater.
- **DROSHKY:** A simple, low, open-topped vehicle once common in Russia.
- **LANDAU:** A carriage with a fully collapsible roof (i.e., a convertible).
- **BROUGHAM:** A light, boxy, enclosed carriage with a front window for passengers.

Stadium *vs.* Arena

Stadiums are large, open venues for field sports like football and baseball.

Arenas are smaller, closed venues for court and rink sports like basketball and hockey.

What About Domes?

Some stadiums are admittedly closed, but unlike most arenas, their ceilings are high-vaulted and/or skylit to preserve an open aesthetic or provide clearance for fly balls. In other words, they have domes.

Pidgin *vs.* Creole

Pidgins are simple hybrid languages that emerge when two groups of people who don't share a common language try to speak to one another.

Creoles are sophisticated hybrid languages that emerge when pidgins grow in complexity and become the native tongue of a speech community.

Making Conversation

Pidgin languages tend to develop in the context of trade between two or more peoples. Pidgins have limited vocabularies and simple grammatical rules—enough to cover basic interactions. No one speaks pidgin as their mother tongue.

Creoles, many linguists believe, develop when children in areas where a pidgin is spoken acquire it in the manner of a mother tongue, expanding its vocabulary and grammar into that of a full-blown language.

However! There's considerable debate on how creoles form, with many linguists contesting the children-who-speak-pidgin hypothesis, otherwise known as the "language bioprogram theory."

A classic example of a pidgin language is Chinese Pidgin English, which emerged in Canton between the British and Chinese in the eighteenth century. The language is thought to have had as few as seven hundred words, including the word *pidgin* itself, which is CPE for the English word business—the whole point of the language in the first place.

With approximately eleven million native speakers, Haitian Creole (Kreyòl Ayisyen) has the most first-language speakers of any creole in the world. A hybrid of French, Fongbe, Igbo, and a handful of related West African languages of the Volta-Congo language branch, Kreyòl is one of the two official languages of Haiti (along with French) and the first language of roughly 95 percent of the population. Despite the abstract definition of creole given above, it's worth noting that most creole languages emerged in the seventeenth and eighteenth centuries in the interaction between European colonists and African slaves, and the term is inseparable from this history.

What About Patois?

Unlike pidgins and creoles, which result from the interaction of two or more languages, patois refers to a nonstandard variant of a single language family, especially a rural or provincial one. Unfortunately, the term is sometimes used as a slur by big-city snobs who think they speak "proper" French or English as opposed to whatever it is they speak out in the boonies. Less haughty types, however, appreciate these languages for what they are: not as aberrations of a standard, but as siblings within the same family. Picard (or Ch'ti) in the north of France is a classic example, as are the many dialects of Low German (or Plattdüütsch) in the north of Germany and northeastern Netherlands.

To confuse matters a bit, the word patois is also used in reference to certain creole languages, as for example Jamaican Patwah or Macanese Patuá, despite the fact that they are not patois as defined above. More confusingly still, the term patois is also used to characterize certain experiences of jargon or slang—especially when there's so much of it that it feels like a foreign language.

Because of its many meanings, not to mention judgy overtones, patois is a term largely avoided by modern linguists.

Crew Cut *vs.* Brush Cut *vs.* Buzz Cut

Crew cuts are short on the sides and a bit longer on top, as typical of rowing (aka crew) team members.

Brush cuts are short all around, sort of like a brush.

Buzz cut is an umbrella term, but it usually suggests the latter—there's more buzzing, after all.

Sleet vs. Hail

Sleet forms when snow melts and then refreezes while falling, creating translucent little ice pellets.

Hail forms when updrafts raise water droplets to high altitudes, where they freeze and fall to the ground. Hailstones are larger and more opaque.

Up in the Clouds

When snowflakes fall through a layer of warm air and melt, then through a layer of cold air and refreeze, you get sleet. Sleet pellets make a gentle tapping sound when they land and are a borderline-lovely wintertime thing.

Hail is the opposite of lovely. When storm clouds loft moisture to their highest and coldest regions, those droplets freeze and gain mass before starting to fall, only to repeat the cycle again (getting bigger each time) before their gravity proves too much for the updraft and they hurtle menacingly to the ground, laying waste to windshields and roof shingles everywhere. Hail occurs during thunderstorms, usually in the summer. The worse the storm, the bigger the hailstone.

Slapstick *vs.* Screwball

Slapstick is exaggerated physical comedy.

Screwball is exaggerated rom-com.

Blunt Objects and Blunter Statements

Slapstick trades in props, pratfalls, physical gags, and quasi-violent mishaps. The term derives from a bludgeon used in Italian commedia dell'arte theater that would make a loud noise when it struck you in the backside.

Screwball takes the rom-com genre and goes heavy on the *com*. Rather than start with personality differences that resolve all lovey-dovey, screwball comedies are epic battles of the sexes, satirizing traditional romance plotlines with a less sentimental kind of love story. They feature brash female characters, bizarre situations, and irreverent dialogue cranked up to a rat-a-tat pace.

A uniquely visual form of comedy, slapstick had its heyday in the silent era. A uniquely chatty form of comedy, screwball had its heyday right after that.

"I need him like the ax needs the turkey."

—Barbara Stanwyck in *The Lady Eve*

SLAPSTICK

- Charlie Chaplin
- Buster Keaton
- The Three Stooges
- Laurel & Hardy
- Looney Tunes
- Michael Richards (Kramer)

SCREWBALL

- *It Happened One Night* (1934)
- *Bringing Up Baby* (1938)
- *His Girl Friday* (1940)
- *The Lady Eve* (1941)

You've Got Mail (1998), *Intolerable Cruelty* (2002), and *How to Lose a Guy in 10 Days* (2003) are modern-day rom-coms with screwball elements.

Electric *vs.* Electronic

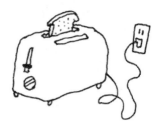

ELECTRIC

Electric devices convert electricity into other forms of energy (heat, light, etc.).

ELECTRONIC

Electronic devices manipulate electricity to convey different kinds of information (images, sounds, etc.).

When Power Becomes Signal

Electric devices (like lamps, toasters, and hair dryers) convert electricity into nonelectrical forms of energy: light, heat, motion, you name it. Because their main goal is some form of power, electric devices tend to rely on highly conductive materials like copper and aluminum—something that will transmit as much energy as possible.

Electronic devices, by contrast, use *semi*conductors like silicon to allow for the more fine-tuned manipulation of electricity in the form of signals that it can interpret and/or amplify (as with radios, telephones, and televisions). Put differently, electronic devices use electricity as a *medium*, processing and relaying information from mic to speaker, camera to screen, keyboard to computer, etc. Devices like these allow us to exert more precise control over electricity—allowing us to play it, as it were, like a violin.

In technical terms, electric devices use passive components like resistors, capacitors, and inductors, while electronic devices introduce active components like transistors, diodes, and rectifiers for greater control over the flow of electrons. As you can see, things get complicated quickly. But the name should at least give us a hint: Nodding to its namesake, the electron, electronics concerns the flow of electricity at a more granular level.

Satin *vs.* Sateen

Satin is very smooth and very shiny.

Sateen is somewhat smooth and somewhat shiny.

Fabrics Up Close

Contrary to popular belief, satin isn't a fabric: It's a weave. In fact, satin is considered one of the three basic kinds of weave—alongside plain weave and twill—and it gets its signature sheen from the way that weave is woven. Unlike plain weaves, whose crisscrossing threads come together in a simple, one-over-one-under pattern, satin floats over a full four threads or more before ducking under one. And the effect of lining up so many yarns together is to reflect the light more evenly. The trade-off? Satin's more vulnerable to snags.

As for sateen, the two fabrics are pretty much identical as far as weave goes, interlaced according to a similar 4/1 base pattern of warp over weft or weft over warp. Where they differ, however, is in their source material: Satin is made of silk, nylon, polyester, or some other fiber of continuous length—what weavers call filament fiber—whereas sateen is made of discontinuous or "staple" fibers that must be spun into a continuous yarn before they're suitable for weaving; think cotton, linen, or really any natural fiber other than silk. Because of the inherent reflectivity of filament, satin tends to be the shinier of the two.

Satin is common in upscale upholstery and ball gowns, while sateen is more common in bedding and drapery. And just to note: Satin isn't always the better choice. Cotton is more breathable than synthetics, and more durable and washable than silk, so really, it depends on your needs.

Twill, to complete our tour of basic weaves, is characterized less by the

PLAIN   TWILL   SATIN

number of threads floating over and under each other than by the fact that, from one row to the next, the starting point moves forward by one. The result? Telltale diagonal lines or "ribs" such as are generally found on jeans. That being said, twill typically follows a 2/1, 3/1, or 2/2 pattern—basically anything between the simple perpendicularity of a plain weave and the parallel-dominant evenness of satin. Twill that changes direction at regular intervals to create a recurring chevron pattern is called herringbone.

Valid *vs.* Sound

All humans are green. **I am a human.**	**All humans are mortal.** **I am a human.**
———————————	———————————
Therefore, I am green.	**Therefore, I am mortal.**
VALID	SOUND
Valid arguments are consistent.	Sound arguments are consistent and correct.

Making Your Point

In the field of logic, validity simply means that the conclusion follows from the premises. It doesn't actually say anything about whether those premises are true.

Soundness, by contrast, refers to arguments that are (1) valid and (2) have true premises, combining to ensure that the conclusions are also true.

One benefit of the distinction between validity and soundness is that it lets you explain precisely why your friend is wrong. If their conclusion doesn't follow from their premises, their argument is invalid. If their reasoning is solid but their facts are just plain wrong, their argument is valid but unsound. And if their facts are wrong *and* their conclusion doesn't follow from them, they're just really bad at arguing.

Keep in mind that these terms only apply to cases of deductive reasoning, where the goal is to derive logical certainties. Where reasoning is inductive, or makes generalizations of greater or lesser probability, an argument can never be perfectly valid or invalid but only strong or weak: The premises support, or fail to support, the likelihood that a given conclusion is true.

Couch *vs.* Sofa

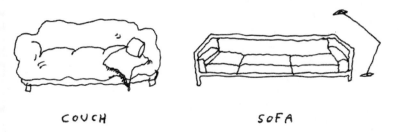

COUCH   SOFA

Couch brings to mind a comfy and casual lounger, while sofa suggests something more elegant and upright.

Beyond this faint connotation, the words are basically interchangeable. Unless you're using sofa as shorthand for "sofa bed," which is, of course, synonymous with "pullout couch."

Monk *vs.* Friar

Monks live in monasteries.   Friars don't.

Articles of Faith

Christian monks live in closed communities where they lead a life of prayer, study, and manual labor. They are effectively cut off from society.

Friars, by contrast, live among laypeople to wander, preach, serve the community, and lead a life of poverty subsidized by alms. They belong not to monastic, but to mendicant (begging) orders like the Franciscans and the Dominicans. Many historical figures commonly thought of as monks (at least by me) were, in fact, friars, including:

- Thomas Aquinas (theologian)
- Martin Luther (Protestant reformer)
- Roger Bacon (protoscientist/wizard)
- Meister Eckhart (mystic)
- William of Ockham (razor guy)

The female counterparts to monks and friars are, respectively, nuns and sisters—another commonly confused pair.

Similar religious orders can be found in Buddhism, Hinduism, Jainism, and other faiths around the world.

MONK / FRIAR

Kink *vs.* Fetish

A kink is an unconventional sexual preference.

A fetish is an unconventional sexual requirement.

Wanting to touch someone's feet is a kink.
If you can't be aroused otherwise, it's a fetish.

Looking for Love

Strictly speaking, a fetish is an object or body part (other than the genitals) on which the fetishist is fixated, but the term is commonly used to refer to activities, too. What ultimately differentiates a kink from a fetish is simply whether it's desired for arousal or *required* for arousal.

Common kinks and fetishes include:

- BDSM
- Role-playing
- Voyeurism
- Exhibitionism
- Shoe fetishism
- Foot partialism
- Leather

Note that any of these may qualify as a fetish or kink today, but what counts as unconventional changes with the times.

KINK / FETISH

Pronunciation *vs.* Enunciation

Actually, it's
/ˈno͞oklēər/.

Huh? I didn't
quite catch you.

PRONUNCIATION

ENUNCIATION

To pronounce a word is to say it correctly.

To enunciate a word is to say it clearly.

One has to do with using the right phonemes.
The other has to do with not mumbling.

Hors d'Oeuvre *vs.* Canapé

HORS D'OEUVRE

CANAPÉ

Hors d'oeuvres are bite-size appetizers.

Canapés are bite-size appetizers on bread, crackers, or pastry.

Finger Foods

Either of these may appear outside of cocktail hour—in a restaurant, for instance—but standing rooms are their main stage. Crudités, or raw vegetables with dip, are another classic (though less appealing) hors d'oeuvre. The term *amuse-bouche*, finally, refers to any hors d'oeuvre consisting of a single bite and which the chef imposes on you without your consent.

Umlaut *vs.* Dieresis

über

UMLAUT

Umlauts give vowels a more *e*-like pronunciation.

naïve

DIERESIS

Diereses indicate that a new syllable has begun.

Double Dots

The umlaut and dieresis look identical but do different things. Umlauts appear in German to indicate that the vowel gets a more "fronted" or *e*-like sound, as when the /oh/ in Schon becomes an /oe/ in Schön, or when the /ah/ in Hand becomes an /eh/ in Hände. The dieresis (*dy-ERR-uh-sis*), by contrast, appears in French to indicate that the vowel is pronounced separately from what preceded it so that we don't pronounce naïve like knave.

Other languages that use umlauts include Azerbaijani, Estonian, Finnish, Hungarian, Slovak, Swedish, and Turkish. Other languages that use diereses include Afrikaans, Catalan, Dutch, Galician, Spanish, Ukrainian, and Welsh. In English, a few lingering diereses exist but are largely optional, as with naïve, Zoë, Chloë, Noël, Brontë (mandatory), and, if you're a copyeditor at *The New Yorker*, coöperate. The accents in Häagen-Dazs, Mötley Crüe, Blue Öyster Cult, Motörhead, and, most endearingly, Sp ̇nal Tap (with an impossible accent over the *n* and, even better, a dotless *i*) are purely ornamental. The word *tréma*, finally, means "dieresis" in French, but in English may refer to diereses or to the double-dotted accent regardless of its function.

Tremolo *vs.* Vibrato

—— —— —— —— —— $\sim\sim\sim\sim\sim\sim\sim$

TREMOLO VIBRATO

Tremolo is oscillating volume. Vibrato is oscillating pitch.

Playing With Sound

Tremolo sounds halting, or in and out. "How Soon Is Now" by The Smiths is a classic example, as is "Bang Bang" by Nancy Sinatra.

Vibrato sounds warbly, or up and down. Think B. B. King blues riffs, or any opera solo you've ever heard.

Tremolo can be produced via pedal or amp, as in the examples above, or achieved manually (and much more sharply) by a rapid plucking of the guitar string or back-and-forth of the violin bow—think suspenseful movie scenes or Dick Dale's rendition of "Miserlou" as popularized in *Pulp Fiction*. Vibrato, by contrast, is achieved by wobbling your hand over the fretboard or bending the string up and down; it's particularly prevalent in singing, where the volume may modulate a little as well. Both tremolo and vibrato are employed widely across instruments and genres.

The whammy bar on a guitar, finally, is misleadingly also called a tremolo arm. By slackening the strings to bend their pitch, what it enables is vibrato.

Gondola *vs.* Funicular

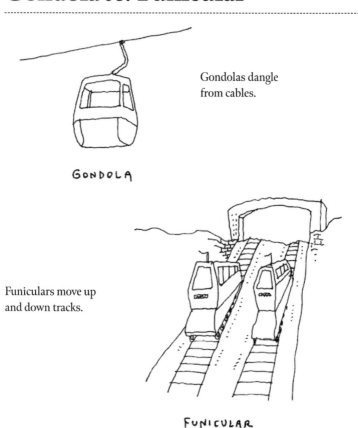

Gondolas dangle from cables.

GONDOLA

Funiculars move up and down tracks.

FUNICULAR

GOING UP?

Both contraptions use cables to move people uphill, but gondolas are suspended by them and move in a continuous loop, while funiculars use them to create a counterweight system of two cars guided by tracks: one going up, the other down.

Climbing the Mountain

Aerial Tramway

The finer difference, really, lies between gondolas and aerial tramways. Rather than loop in a circle like gondolas, aerial tramways shuttle back and forth in a straight line. And while gondolas move continuously, scooping people up as they go, aerial tramways come to a complete stop at either end. They also hold a lot more people. Cable car is a third (and frustratingly ambiguous) term that may refer to either device, or even to certain non-aerial tramway systems like those in San Francisco. They all use cables, after all.

Finally, while we're here: Chairlifts are open gondolas.

Inclined Elevator

Funiculars, finally, may be distinguished from inclined elevators, which don't use the aforementioned counterweight system but are basically just elevators that go up and down at an angle. Still, many inclined elevators around the world are misleadingly termed "funiculars," perhaps because it's fun to say. Paris's Montmartre Funicular, for instance, is a set of inclined elevators; they just kept the name from when it used to be a you-know-what.

Schlemiel *vs.* Schlimazel

Schlemiels are bumbling fools.   Schlimazels have bad luck.

Hence the Yiddish crack that when a schlemiel spills their soup,
it's the schlimazel whose lap it falls on.

Sad Sacks

With schlemiels and schlimazels, we may distinguish between two kinds of loser.

Schlemiels are clumsy, foolish, and loudly incompetent. *Seinfeld*'s Kramer and *Broad City*'s Ilana Glazer are typical schlemiels: Through inane scheming and oafish ineptitude, they bring trouble upon themselves and those around them.

In the blast radius of every schlemiel, by contrast, lies the hapless schlimazel—folks like Kramer's George or Ilana's Abbi. Their bad luck tends to happen *to* them, whether by virtue of a nearby you-know-who or because it's simply their fate.

In short, schlemiels are active screw-ups whose idiotic plans always spell disaster, while shlimazels (literally, "bad luck" in Yiddish) are born losers who always get the short end of the stick.

Poisonous *vs.* Venomous

POISONOUS

Poison is when you bite it.

VENOMOUS

Venom is when it bites you.

The Fine Print

Poison is passively delivered: You eat, drink, touch, or inhale something that was minding its own business and the results are memorably unpleasant.

Venom is actively delivered: An animal that doesn't particularly care for you injects you with their particular brand of toxin via fang, stinger, or, in the case of the platypus, heel spur.

Swamp *vs.* Marsh *vs.* Bog

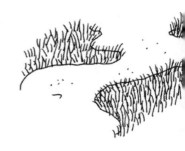

SWAMP

Swamps are woody.

MARSH

Marshes are grassy.

BOG

Bogs are mossy.

Wetland Ways

Neither terrestrial nor aquatic, wetlands are naturally a bit tricky when it comes to clear-cut definition. Swamps are riddled with trees and wooded shrubs, while marshes are all soft-stemmed grass and reed. Bogs, meanwhile, are highly acidic, so they don't grow much besides mosses and heathers, which leave behind a spongy, slowly decaying plant matter called peat. Fens, the unsung wetland of the four classic types, are peaty like bogs, only they're not so acidic, so more can grow there.

Beautiful *vs.* Sublime

BEAUTIFUL

Beauty is pleasing.

SUBLIME

The sublime is awe-inspiring.

Meadows and sunsets are beautiful.
Thunderstorms and meteor showers are sublime.

The Perfect *vs.* the Infinite

In aesthetic theory, beauty is often characterized by harmony, balance, completeness, and proportion. The sublime, by contrast, refers to an excess *beyond* such ratios—the incalculable, the staggering, the mighty and magnificent. In short: The beautiful delights us, while the sublime overwhelms.

> *"If he could feel the beauty of Genoa . . .*
> *he must necessarily be conscious of the sublimity of Manhattan."*
>
> —William McFee, *Aliens*

Notes

Page 1 (Emoji, Emoticon): Despite its use of a Japanese character,
ˉ_(ツ)_/ˉ is less typical of kaomoji style. More characteristic
kaomoji include (^_^), (*_*), (●　●✿), and (づ ￣ ³ ￣)づ . Also of
note, the flipping table: (╯°□°）╯︵ ┻━┻

Page 2 (Symphony, Concerto): Concertos may feature more than one
soloist, e.g., Bach's Concerto for Two Violins in D Minor.

Page 6 (Great Britain, United Kingdom): The United Kingdom is short for
the United Kingdom of Great Britain and Northern Ireland, although
in addition to this island-and-a-fifth the nation includes hundreds of
smaller islets like England's Isle of Wight and Scotland's Hebrides,
Orkney, and Shetland islands—none of which are technically part of
the Great Britain landmass but which are politically intended by the
term. Annoyingly, Britain, British, etc., can refer either to Great Britain
or to the UK. Usually the latter. Like Great Britain, Ireland is a landmass rather than a unified political entity, though not without conflict
over the matter. Its political constituents are Northern Ireland to the
north (already discussed) and the much larger Republic of Ireland to
the south, an independent nation. All islands in the area—including
Great Britain, Ireland, the smaller UK isles mentioned above, as well
as the three self-governing Crown Dependencies known as the Isle of
Man, Jersey, and Guernsey—are collectively called the British Isles.
We call the biggest of them "great" to distinguish it from its smaller
sibling, Ireland, although some argue that the smaller sibling is really
Brittany in France. Both have been called "Little Britain" at various
points in history.

Page 8 (Envy, Jealousy): In his 1816 *Dictionary of English Synonymes*, George
Crabb summarized it well: "We are jealous of what is our own; we are
envious of what is another's. Jealousy fears to lose what it has; envy is
pained at seeing another have that which it wants for itself."

Page 9 (Bay, Gulf, Cove): Drawing on examples of narrow inlets like the Persian Gulf or the Gulf of Thailand, some writers claim that the difference between a bay and a gulf has to do with shape as much as size—i.e., that gulfs are narrower or more recessed while bays are wider or more open—but the wide-mouthed gulfs of Alaska, Guinea, and Tehuantepec suggest otherwise. Or are they the exception to the rule? And then there's the Bay of Bengal and Hudson Bay, which are as big as any gulf, although the latter is usually classified not as a gulf but an inland sea. So really, it's a bit of a mess. At best we can say that, with some exception, bays tend to be smaller and wide-mouthed, while gulfs are larger but more varied in shape. Coves, meanwhile, tend to look scooped out, with rising, amphitheater-like walls. They're very charming.

Page 10 (Latte, Flat White, Cappuccino, Cortado): On the subject of textured milk: It has to be admitted that *some* surface foam will resist blending and sit on top from the beginning. But still, it's not like the old days, where a cappuccino's surface foam was the main event. With modern cappuccinos and flat whites, the real foam lies within.

Page 22 (Shame, Guilt): Like guilt, shame can admittedly pertain to actions or thoughts and not just your innate qualities; but even then, the emphasis tends to be on who you are rather than on what you did (*guilty for stealing, shame for being a thief*). For an interesting analysis of the difference between shame and guilt, see Maria Miceli and Cristiano Castelfranchia, "Reconsidering the Differences Between Shame and Guilt," *Europe's Journal of Psychology* 14, no. 3 (August 2018), 710–733.

Page 28 (Snitch, Rat): "Snitches and rats are not the same thing. Let me break it down to make sure y'all see what I mean. A snitch is someone minding other folks' business to find information they can sell for a price or trade for some other form of compensation. A rat is a traitor, a conceiver, planner, or physical participator. He doesn't sell secrets for power or cash—he betrays the trust of his team or his family, hoping to save his own cowardly ass . . ." —Morgan Freeman in "Snitches & Rats (Interlude)" by 21 Savage and Metro Boomin. TV shows and films cited: *The Wire, The Sopranos, The Departed, The Matrix, The Godfather, Reservoir Dogs,* and *Recess*.

Page 30 (Epigram, Aphorism, Maxim, Adage, Proverb): There are also verse epigrams and legal maxims, but these are beyond our scope. Maxim may also refer to a general principle more broadly, not necessarily one indicating a rule of conduct. "Proverbs are maxims of the people." —John Trusler, *The Difference between Words Esteemed Synonymous in the English Language,* 1766.

Page 32 (Natural Numbers, Integers, Rational Numbers, Real Numbers): Rather than try to remember all of the different number categories, a good way to think about it is through opposition: At the highest level, you've got real vs imaginary numbers. Then, within the vastly more useful world of real numbers, you've got rational vs. irrational numbers (those that can and cannot be reduced to ratios of two numbers). Within the world of rational numbers, finally, just look at the words themselves: You've got "integers," which are "entire" in the sense that they don't include fractions. As for "natural" numbers, have you ever seen negatives in nature?

Page 34 (Squash, Racquetball): Squash and racquetball have also evolved three-player versions.

Page 36 (Flail, Mace, Morning Star): Japanese nunchaku (nunchucks) are thought by many to derive from rice-threshing flails.

Page 40 (Amp, Volt, Watt): Electricity isn't just pushed by an energy source—it's also pulled by it, making voltage more accurately a measure of the differential pressure or tension created between the negative (push) and positive (pull) charges that combine to thread energy through your device. If it does so in one continuous loop (as with batteries), it's called a direct current (DC), while if it's more of a jiggly back-and-forth action (as with plug outlets), it's called an alternating current (AC). I also didn't discuss ohms, which is really the final piece of the puzzle as it measures electrical resistance, whether in terms of the width and length of the wire, the limits of conductivity of the wire's material, or the resistive force of the device you're powering. Think of resistance as a kind of counterforce to pressure: the volts push the amps, the ohms push back, and the result is the amount you actually get. You can calculate resistance by dividing volts by amps.

Page 42 (Sorbet, Sherbet): FDA regulation stipulates that sherbet must contain between 1 and 2% milkfat, while ice cream must contain no less than 10% milkfat, leaving us all to wonder: What lies in between the two? It's an uncanny valley of frozen dairy. In the UK, meanwhile, sherbet refers to a sweet fizzy powder that you can mix with water or dip other sweets into. Sort of like Fun Dip, but fizzy. Honestly, it sounds quite good.

Page 44 (Convince, Persuade): Both convince and persuade may safely be paired with "that."

Page 52 (Club Soda, Sparkling Water, Seltzer): The spring water from which Perrier derives is naturally carbonated; these days, however, the water is purified and then manually re-carbonated for consistency. The spring water from which San Pellegrino derives is not naturally carbonated.

Page 54 (Hermit, Anchorite): The *OED* allows that anchorite can mean "a person who has withdrawn or secluded him or herself from the world, usually for religious reasons; a recluse, a hermit," making the two words effectively synonymous. But that strikes me as untidy—the walled-in recluse is a special type of ascetic and deserves its own word.

Page 56 (Maze, Labyrinth): For further discussion on the historical discrepancy between written descriptions of the labyrinth as many-pathed (or multicursal) and its visual depiction on coins and mosaics as single-pathed (or unicursal), see Penelope Reed Doob, *The Idea of the Labyrinth from Classical Antiquity Through the Middle Ages* (Ithaca, NY: Cornell University Press, 1990). Also, yes, technically, mazes can have centers as their goal (e.g., England's Hampton Court Maze).

Page 58 (All-Wheel Drive, Four-Wheel Drive): Despite their primary differences, individual automakers may use these terms idiosyncratically or devise their own language (e.g., Mercedes's 4Matic, Jeep's 4x4). As technology has improved over the years, two-wheel drive has also developed its own forms of traction control. As for remembering which is which: *All*-wheel drive is *always* on, while *four*-wheel drive indicates that you've switched on a mode in a car that's normally *two*-wheel drive.

Page 62 (Spear, Javelin, Lance, Pike): The line-formation pike eventually evolved into the bayonet.

Page 69 (Shotgun House, Railroad Apartment): Although tenement buildings were prevalent in other large North American cities like Chicago and Boston, nowhere on the continent had more of them than New York City.

Page 72 (Combination, Permutation): How many two-digit combinations can you form out of the numbers 1, 2, and 3? The answer is 3: 12, 13, and 23. How many two-digit *permutations* can you form? The answer is 6: 12, 13, 23, 32, 31, and 21. Note that with permutations, the order can be spatial, as with a seating plan, or *temporal*, as with the order in which dishes are served.

Page 78 (Crypt, Catacomb): Church crypts need not house the dead but may store holy relics or feature additional chapels instead—though relics, in part or in whole, are often dead people, too. The term crypt may also be used more broadly to refer to any enclosed burial chamber, not just those under churches or even those underground, so long as they're hidden in some way, e.g., mausoleum crypts and wall crypts.

Page 80 (Lager, Ale): The strain of yeast typically used to make lager is *Saccharomyces pastorianus*, while that for ale is *Saccharomyces cerevisiae*. In the world of brewing, these are often classed as bottom-fermenting and top-fermenting yeasts, respectively, based on how they'd sink or rise in the fermentation vessel and where you'd collect them from. These days, however, modern brewing equipment generally requires that the yeast be collected from the bottom regardless of its strain, making the terms a matter of tradition more than anything else. *Lager* comes from the German word meaning "to store," which is what you have to do to make it. In fact, the long cold storage (or lagering) of the beer following fermentation helps to further clarify and smooth out the flavor. For ale, this kind of conditioning is optional. Given their time and temperature requirements, lagers are generally the harder beer to brew. The short turnarounds and experimental leeway of ale, by contrast, are what make it the darling of the craft brew industry.

Page 92 (Strategy, Tactics): "I propose to define strategy in general (and realized strategy in particular) as a pattern in a stream of decisions." —Henry Mintzberg, "Strategy Formulation as a Historical Process," *International Studies of Management & Organization* 7, no. 2 (1977), 28.

Page 96 (Irony, Sarcasm): "Sarcasm does not necessarily involve irony, & irony has often no touch of sarcasm" —H. W. Fowler, *A Dictionary* *of Modern English Usage*, 1st ed. (Oxford, UK: Clarendon Press, 1926), 513. "Sarcasm, 1: a sharp and *often* satirical or ironic utterance designed to cut or give pain. 2a: a mode of satirical wit depending for its effect on bitter, caustic, and *often* ironic language that is usually directed against an individual" —Merriam-Webster.com (emphases mine). "Sarcasm, A sharp, bitter, or cutting expression or remark; a bitter gibe or taunt" —*OED* (no mention of irony).

Page 98 (Doula, Midwife): In the US, licensed midwives actually fall into three categories: certified nurse-midwives (CNMs), whose degree in midwifery is preceded by a degree in nursing; certified midwives (CMs), whose degree in midwifery is *not* preceded by a degree in nursing but who otherwise receive the same graduate-level midwife training; and certified professional midwives (CPMs), whose training in midwifery is not preceded by a degree in nursing and who are trained specifically for out-of-hospital births. The latter two are licensed to practice only in certain states.

Page 102 (Hue, Tint, Shade, Tone): Often used interchangeably with chroma, saturation measures the amount of chroma in a hue *relative* to its value, so it's a bit more complicated. The language of tints, tones, and shades comes from the world of painting and in particular paint mixing.

Page 112 (Jargon, Slang): Jargon and slang can and often do occur in the same sentence, as when snowboarders (I imagine) say things like "Way to stomp that lipslide" (stomp being slang, lipslide jargon). Office talk is rife with both, and it can be hard to draw a line between them. Is *bandwidth* slang for availability, or is it jargon for something more specific—availability *to do work*? Finally, it's worth noting that slang is predominantly spoken (or texted) and constantly changing, while jargon skews toward the written and evolves more slowly.

Page 114 (Stock, Bond): I said that stocks represent ownership of a company, but strictly speaking, what stocks do is entitle you to a portion of the company's profits in the form of dividends; to the cash value of its assets (less its liabilities) in the event of bankruptcy; and to certain voting rights. That is the essential basis on which shares have their value in the market.

Page 132 (Civil Law, Common Law): Confusingly, the term civil law is also used *within* the world of common law to refer to cases concerning private relationships and property—i.e., as opposed to criminal law. A different sense of the term entirely.

Page 140 (EST, EDT, ET): Needless to say, EST/EDT is just one example. For Pacific Time (PT), Mountain Time (MT), New Zealand Time (NZT), or indeed anywhere else daylight saving time is observed, the idea is the same: In spring you "spring forward" an hour and add a D, while in fall you "fall back" to the standard and swap in an S, though exact dates and times (and naming conventions) vary by region, especially as you jump hemispheres. In North America, standard time (whether EST, CST, AST, etc.) used to cover half the year, then went down to five months in the eighties, and, as of 2007–2008, is almost as short as four, covering the first Sunday of November to the second Sunday of March. In other words, daylight saving time is eating up more and more of our year, and indeed many anti-tinker movements are in favor of switching completely to DST rather than back to the old standard. As for the fate of such movements, time, literally, will tell.

Page 154 (Hansom, Barouche, Stagecoach, Troika): Though often built as sleds, troikas may also be equipped with wheels.

Page 158 (Pidgin, Creole): Aside from its linguistic meaning, creole also refers to individuals of European, African, and/or mixed descent

who were born in the West Indies and colonial Americas—
especially those with long family histories in the area—as opposed
to those who immigrated there. This sense of the word is highly
regionalized, however, and means one thing in Suriname and
another in French Guiana, while in Louisiana it means different
things to different groups. The term is also used in Mauritius and a
handful of other Indian Ocean nations.

Page 175 (Tremolo, Vibrato): The rapid plucks and bow-strokes of manual
tremolo are admittedly better described as "repetitive" or even
"percussive" than simply as oscillations in volume. But these are
oscillations of a more extreme type: In and out is sharpened to on
and off.

Page 176 (Gondola, Funicular): The boats used in Venice are also called
gondolas. They're something else entirely.

Index

Acknowledgments

Joy Tutela, Jay Sacher, Avia Wiseman, Ruth Burnstein, Marcus Burnstein, Jessica Burnstein, Evan Middleton, Jay Bhatti, Nora Newhouse, James Camp, Luke Fentress, Giuseppe Castellano, Tyler Cohen, Phil Underwood, Kasia Mychajlowycz, Dr. Tom Murad, Matthew Jacobs, Laura Serejo Genes, David Gruber, Kevin Zheng, Claire Fauquier, Noah Epstein, Nikki Gershbain, Kavita Joshi, Andrew Shinewald, Miguel Narvaez, James Anagnoson, Peter Simon, Patrick Pittman, Howard Epstein, Linda Epstein, John Di Palma, Kelly Kwan, Ivy McFadden, Diana Drew, Melissa Farris, Quote Investigator, and the team at Ethica Coffee Roasters in Toronto.

UNION SQUARE & CO.

NEW YORK

Copyright *vs.* Trademark

COPYRIGHT

Copyright protects an
author's original work.

TRADEMARK

Trademarks protect a
company's identifying marks.

One applies to movies, music, and books,
the other to brand names, logos, and slogans.

The *Actual* Fine Print

Copyrights and trademarks protect intellectual property, but in different ways. Copyright prohibits others from reproducing, distributing, performing, displaying, or adapting original works of authorship without the creator's permission, essentially to ensure that they're paid for their work. Copyrighted works include novels, plays, songs, paintings, photographs, screenplays, and so on. In the US, copyright is granted automatically upon creation (publication isn't required) and lasts for the creator's life plus seventy years. Importantly, you cannot copyright an idea, only its expression in tangible media.

Trademarks, by contrast, prevent others in the same industry from adopting the same name, logo, or other identifying mark to preserve brand integrity, ward off counterfeits, and generally indicate goods or services as coming from a particular source. In addition to names, logos, and slogans, trademarks can include jingles, animations, colors, sounds, and even scents.

TM

UNREGISTERED TRADEMARK

Like copyrights, trademarks don't technically require registration: They are granted the moment you begin using distinct symbols to identify your business's goods or services.

However! Unregistered trademarks afford fewer protections and are harder to enforce than registered ones, which is why many businesses will register their trademarks with the United States Patent and Trademark Office or their nation's equivalent, upgrading Billy's Hats™ to Billy's Hats® (*R* stands for "registered"). Unlike copyright, registered trademarks last forever, provided they remain in use and are renewed at regular intervals.